The *breakup* survival guide for women

How to Heal Your Broken Heart, Achieve Closure, and Get On with Your Life

Susanna Gold

ISBN: 978-1-98-672842-3

2nd Edition
Cover Illustration: Kachaev
Book Cover: Christine's Cover Designs
Createspace, Charleston SC

To my sister Rachel, whose support and opinions were invaluable in the writing of this book.

Table of Contents

Introduction

As someone who has suffered from a broken heart, I know the pain of having to carry on when you can't be with the person you love. I had loved and lost over the years, and each time I struggled to recover. But there was one breakup that was far more devastating than the others. After this incredibly painful breakup, I was at a crossroads. I had suffered for nearly a year, unable to accept the end of my relationship. But I knew that if I didn't make a strong and genuine effort to recover, I would continue to be depressed and find little joy in life. I didn't want to become bitter, so I decided to try my best to be positive. It was difficult, but I found that the positive attitude I portrayed on the outside soon became how I felt on the inside. As I struggled to come to terms with my loss, I came up with techniques and solutions that were effective at lifting me out of depression and easing me into my new life without my ex. I would like to share them with you. By learning from my mistakes and remaining optimistic, I was able to get over my breakup and finally meet the right person who I had been searching for most of my life.

If you are struggling to get over a breakup, feeling emotionally drained and as if you might never fully recover, this book will be of great help to you. It offers innovative ways in which to direct your time and energy while rebuilding your confidence, so that you will be able to pull yourself out of your negative state of mind, and begin to function again. It will enable you to learn lessons from your breakup, find constructive ways to cope with your feelings, and achieve closure. You will learn how to:

- Accept the end of the relationship.
- Keep yourself from contacting your ex.
- Avoid stress during the healing process.
- Grieve properly and immediately after the breakup so that you don't get stuck in an endless cycle of grieving.
- Analyze and review what happened during your relationship so that you can achieve closure on your own.
- Live in the present and look towards the future instead of obsessing about the past.
- Avoid denigrating yourself and gain your confidence back.

Summaries serve as reminders after each chapter – if you feel the need, you can refer to them whenever necessary. Everyone heals at a different pace. Although the book moves rapidly, don't feel that you must follow a specific time frame. My hope is that you will get to a healthy place emotionally after your breakup, as soon as possible.

- Susanna Gold

Chapter One

Accepting That It's Over

Breakups are traumatic, life-changing events. When you realize that your relationship is over, it's devastating. There may be moments when you feel sheer desperation. You want him back so badly that the pain is unbearable. You feel completely alone and helpless because there seems to be nothing you can do to make yourself feel better. You analyze every moment of your time with him to the point of exhaustion. You see the world through a gray fog, and it's impossible to concentrate at work or socialize in any genuine way. You try your best to be strong, but the devastation takes its toll; you feel calm and composed one minute, and distressed the next. Everything reminds you of him. Movies and television shows with tragic romantic plots seem like they were written solely for you. You relate intensely to the characters, feeling their pain and comparing it to your own. Certain parts of town become no-go areas because you went there with him. You attach memories to every store you entered and every restaurant you frequented as a couple. When you do decide to go to these places, memories overwhelm you. You look around; everyone seems to be behaving normally and going about their business as usual. It is a surreal experience because there is vibrant energy humming all around you, yet you feel like your world has come to an abrupt halt. You almost feel like a ghost that no one can see, or a victim of an accident who is being ignored. You want to ask people for help, but you know that no one else has that ability - the only one who can save you from your pain is yourself.

During your relationship, you dreamed of a bright future; waking up every morning next to him, the friends you shared, the world that you built around him. Unfortunately, no matter how much you care for another person, you have no power over their decisions or actions. You cannot demand that he work on fixing your relationship or that he come back. The fact that you miss him and want him back is understandable. However, waiting patiently for his return instead of moving forward with your life will only prolong your pain. You could end up wasting months or even years, endlessly waiting. The hope for reconciliation will have you living in a parallel universe - wanting him back while at the same time, wanting to get over him, two conflicting emotions. The only way to get over the breakup is to accept that he is not coming back and make decisions in your life reflecting this.

Remove the Pedestal and Stop Telling Yourself That He Was "The One"

Ask yourself why you are idealizing this person and putting him on a pedestal. What needs did he fulfill in your life? And, why have you been able to recover from past breakups and disappointments, but not this one? Answer these questions and you are on your way to getting over him. Since he is no longer there, it's important that you be able to fill that emptiness.

Don't sabotage your life by convincing yourself that your ex was perfect in every way, or worse, that he was "the one." When you do this, you are imposing your past on your future. Your future is wide open, so the last thing you should do is write off other men who approach you or place them in a lesser position in your mind. Men who are intuitive will know that something is wrong and will have less incentive to pursue you. Doing this to yourself also blocks you from being open to them, keeping you in a kind of dating purgatory. Don't let the memories of your ex cause you to shut down and reject other people once you're ready to date again. Remain open and embrace the fact that every man you meet will be different.

Have a Plan

The first few weeks after a breakup are the toughest. Getting through each day is an accomplishment, in and of itself. However, if you know *how* to heal, you can minimize the trauma and drastically cut down on the time it takes to recover. If you set your mind to it, and have some guidance and a plan to back you up, you can get to a comfortable place emotionally and heal considerably in a short period of time. But this can only happen if you have a genuine desire to put the relationship behind you. Instead of stagnating and feeling down every day, you want to feel better. The first step is disconnecting yourself from your ex. This means making the firm decision not to contact him. It takes a great deal of strength to control the urge to see him or speak with him. But the earlier you are able to put the relationship behind you the better it will be for you in the long-run.

Don't Call Him

It takes super-human self-control not to call him, especially during the first month after the breakup. The problem with ringing him up or instigating a video call with him is this: If you call him you'll be setting yourself back in the healing process – you will be lengthening the time it takes you to get over him. Hearing the sound of his voice would devastate you and watching him speak to you on video would be even worse. The best way to stop yourself from picking up your phone is to view not doing so as self-protection - you are avoiding pain. Delete his contact information from your cellphone so that the temptation is not directly in front of you all day long.

There's a trick of the mind you can use to keep yourself from calling him; I call it the *Seven-Day Layover*. For this method to work we need a hypothetical situation. Let's say, for example, you are going on a vacation, and while in transit you get stranded at an airport in a foreign city because of a storm. Normally, in real life this would only last a few hours or perhaps a couple of days depending on the severity. But for our purpose, let's say it was a total of seven days. You would be unable to reach your destination and to pass the time you would have to think of things to do to keep yourself occupied.

After the seven-day period, you are informed that you can finally catch a plane that will take you where you want to go. Most people would have one of two reactions: They would go on the trip as planned, or they would be so tuckered-out that they would forgo their trip and head back home to recover. Either way, a decision is being made - to go or not to go. You can use the *Seven-Day Layover* scenario to keep yourself from calling your ex. Here's how: When you're tempted to contact him tell yourself that you'll put him out of your mind for now but will allow yourself to think about him again in one week's time. You are giving yourself a layover period. During this time keep your normal work schedule, plan lots of activities, and go to all your appointments as planned; go about life as usual (as best you can). After this period, allow yourself time to miss him and think about him. You might need an hour or even half a day to reminisce about the relationship - looking at photos, listening to music, or watching films that bring back memories of him, and getting your feelings out. But don't contact him! After taking time to do this, find something else to do and remain busy for the rest of the day. After you get through the first week, give yourself another seven-day period. The week after that, do it again. Gradually, the tension you feel will subside each time you put off the call. As time passes, there will be other pressing issues that pop up in your life and it will be necessary for you to direct your attention away from your ex. Before you know it, a month will have gone by, then two, and then three. You'll be amazed at how well this technique works.

The Social Networks and Messaging App Problem

Once you've deleted your ex from your cellphone he will no longer be on the contacts lists of your messaging apps, so his profile photos will stop popping up. You can also set apps in a way that protects you from outsiders accessing your profile if you wish, so that he can't spy on you if you are worried about this. However, social media is more complex and is constantly evolving. Changes to how these sites operate can and do occur on a regular basis due to regulations and decisions made inside of these companies.

When you were a couple, you may have used social networks to interact with each other. The best way to handle these accounts right after a breakup is to make no changes right away. You should never feel pressured into putting your relationship status up on these sites in the first place, but if you wrote that you had a boyfriend, there is no need to change that information now. Walking away from these networks for several weeks until you get your bearings back would be the healthiest thing for you to do. Only pay attention to any social media you utilize for work so that you don't miss out on anything important. If your family and close friends constantly contact you in this manner, ask them to chat with you using other means until you can gather the strength to change your relationship status, delete your ex's photos, and unfriend or block him. Another thing to remember is that you don't have to be corralled into using these sites. If you don't feel that using a particular site is benefiting you, then stop using it. People open these accounts all the time and they also close them.

The Email Dilemma

If you get a strong urge to email your ex while at work, keep in mind that once an email is sent you can't take it back even if your feelings change later that same day. If you were to get a negative response you would feel hurt, even if you saw it coming. You would be reeling, trying to recover from the blow. Even worse, there's a possibility that you would get no response at all and spend hours or days wondering why, and kicking yourself. To lessen the urge to send him an email, delete emails you've kept on file from him. If you choose, you can block him from emailing you in the future, or if you feel the need, you can delete the email account that he used to contact you on, unless it is work-related.

Don't Convince Yourself That You Need Answers to Your Questions Before You Can Get Over Him

Rarely will someone give you straight answers or admit the real reason why they chose to end a relationship. Contacting him and trying to get those answers will likely be futile. Short of hiring a private investigator, if it was a clear case of infidelity, you will not get the full story. Instead of sitting around feeling desperate, helpless, and wondering *why*, a better thing to do would be to accept that since you won't be getting the information you seek, you will have to get around this problem yourself. You don't need answers directly from him to get over him. You can achieve closure on your own, in your own time, and in your own way. The writing exercise in **Chapter Nine** will help you do that.

Plan Activities to Keep Yourself Busy

It's important to give yourself some relief from the stress that heartbreak brings. Because all of us experience stress differently, we also have different ways of coping. Becoming involved in various activities and performing simple tasks can help keep you from obsessing about him. If you feel the need, make a list that you can refer to when you are tempted to contact him using different tactics such as: Diverting your attention, exercise/exertion, and spirituality/looking inward.

Divert Your Attention

1. Call a friend and talk about subjects other than *him* and keep the conversation going.
2. Enjoy the company of your friends in person, rather than online.

3. Whip up a complicated recipe.
4. Take on an extra project at work or work longer hours.
5. Learn a new language.
6. Shop for a better deal: search for a better rate on car insurance, phone service, and other necessities.
7. Watch a comedy, action, or horror film (romance is out for now).
8. Go to a bookstore, your local library, or search online for titles that peak your interest.
9. Organize your mail, your room, or your weekly schedule.
10. Redecorate a frequently used area of your home.
11. Update your skills for work. Take a class or learn on your own.

Exercise / Exertion

1. Go to the gym and have a workout.
2. Sign up for a self-defense class.
3. Go swimming, play tennis, or whichever sport you enjoy.
4. Take a long walk, run, or go for a bike ride.
5. Instead of taking your car for a wash, do it yourself.
6. Clean the house or do the laundry.

Spirituality / Looking Inward

1. Cuddle your pet.
2. Buy a gift for a friend or family member.
3. Listen to your favorite music.
4. Get in tune with nature: take a walk on the beach or hike up a trail in the woods.
5. Sign up for a yoga class.
6. Unwind and enjoy your favorite tea or coffee.
7. Attend services at your church, temple, or place of worship.
8. Volunteer for charity work. Not only will it make you feel great, but helping the needy will give you your perspective back. However badly you might be feeling at this time, you'll come to your senses when you meet others whose lives are even harder in comparison.

Utilize Your Appointment Book

If you keep an appointment book or maintain one in your cellphone, you can use it for more than just keeping track of your schedule. Here's how: If you are using a book, purchase some highlighting pens. Put a highlight marking over the days that you are overwhelmed by the urge to contact your ex. Then, pencil in what set off those feelings and made you consider contacting him. If you are using your phone you can insert text into your calendar so that if you see a pattern you can do something about it. An example might be: During your relationship you used to have dinner together every Wednesday night, and since the breakup you feel particularly lonely on Wednesdays. Instead of feeling horrible whenever that day rolls around, schedule an activity from your list. Take a class at the gym and get fit while spending time in the company of other people instead of being alone, designate a girls-night-out, or ask a friend what films she likes and invite her to come over and watch them with you. Keep trying out different ideas until you find the ones that are most effective at keeping you occupied.

Vent Your Feelings in Writing

A great way to vent your feelings in a private and deeply personal way is to express them in writing. Writing is especially helpful for people who don't have a close circle of friends with whom they feel comfortable discussing their breakup. If you feel the need, write a letter to him telling him all your feelings. Keep what you've written in a journal and hide it in a secret place or store it on a flash drive. If you don't wish to read it again, tear it out of your journal and throw it away or delete the file at your leisure.

You've Been Able to Get Through Tough Times in the Past. You Can Do It Again.

Try to recall a challenging period in your life. You may have had health problems, bravely went through treatment, and recovered. Or, you had to pass a rigorous exam, and not only passed it, but scored higher than you ever thought possible. Is there something that you were able to do in your life that others were impressed by, and that you, yourself thought was a great achievement? If so, ask yourself how you were able to do it. If you had the strength and determination then, you can find it now. Try to look at getting over your breakup as another challenge. Yes, it is a different sort of challenge, but it can be met. Retrieve that power now. Don't tell yourself you can't. You can.

Breakup Survival Summaries

- Oftentimes, the hope for reconciliation is what keeps people from getting over a breakup. So that you don't waste months or years hoping for his return, start being proactive about healing.
- Take him off the pedestal you've created in your mind. Figure out what needs he fulfilled in your life and fulfill them a different way – start by working on yourself.
- Don't contact your ex in any way; no phone calls, video calls, chats, or emails.
- Delete his number from your cellphone so that you won't see his profile photo on apps or be tempted to start a chat with him.
- Walk away from your social media accounts for several weeks if possible. Change your relationship status, remove his photos, and unfriend him when you are in a better mental state.
- You don't need answers from him to get over him.
- Think of activities to do that will keep you busy when you get a strong urge to contact him. Base your ideas on what you enjoy and what you think will work.
- Use your appointment book or cellphone to document the days and times you feel the strongest temptation to contact him, and try to figure out what triggers it.
- Express yourself in writing, and get your most private thoughts and feelings out of your system.

- Count your achievements. If you've gotten over large hurdles in the past, you can do it again. Look at getting over your broken heart as another of life's challenges.

Chapter Two

Parting with Memorabilia and Dealing with Change

If you have items in your home that your ex gave you or remind you of him laying about such as clothing, his cologne, or dried flowers saved in honor of a special occasion, gather them in one place. These are not just objects. To you they have deep meaning and can greatly affect your state of mind. Holding onto these things will cause you further pain and only serve to remind you of what you already know - that you were once committed to this person. If you have the strength, toss them in the trash bin. If you're not quite ready, the second best thing to do would be to place them in a garbage or grocery bag. The purpose of using a garbage bag is not to make light of, or somehow demean memories associated with these things. It's simply the easiest and quickest way to collect everything in one place, and it can be stored just about anywhere in the house. You can stuff it under the bed, throw it in the back of the closet, or place it in a room you rarely enter until you're over the breakup and can decide what you'd like to keep, and what you want to throw out. If you have photos of him stored on your computer or cellphone, delete them. If you are a sentimental person you might choose to save one photo onto a flash drive and place it inside the bag with everything else. Once you've done this, you might consider some new touches to your home. Make the space where you spend most of your time look different than when you were in a relationship. Some suggestions are:

- Buy some new throw pillows for your bed or sofa in cheerful patterns and colors that reflect your style.
- Change your home décor to make it more *you*.
- Buy new bedding and towels if you attach memories to the old ones.
- Switch around the furniture, buy a new piece, or give away something you don't use.
- Put different artwork up on the walls.
- Clear clutter: get rid of things that crowd your living space or you feel you no longer need.
- Another more drastic option would be relocating. If you've been considering it for a while for various reasons or you have to leave because you were residing at his home, finding a new place to live in a different neighborhood or city might be just the change you need.

Take Things Slow for a While and Set Your Priorities

Once you begin the process of throwing away his things and redecorating, remember that it's not necessary to finish doing everything in one week or even a month. Move forward at own pace, and if making a change upsets you because you aren't ready for it, then stop doing it and give yourself a break. You will likely need to slow down your pace in other aspects of your life as well until you adjust to being single again, and no longer have moments when you feel a strong sense of being alone rather than part of a couple throughout the day. So that you can get your errands done and run your life as normally as possible, in the evenings before going to bed each night, write in a journal or on a piece of paper all the things that you need to get done the next day. Prioritize the most important things by putting them at the top of your list and place the least important at the bottom. Place your list on the bedside table, tape it to the wall, or on the back of a door. Finish doing whatever you're able to do, and if you are too upset on a particular day to do something, reschedule it for a later date. You *can* do everything that needs to be done, but at a slower pace for now. Accepting this will help you better organize your time and allow you to be gentle on yourself while healing.

The Power of a Flower

Greenery creates an uplifting environment and freshens the air. Buy yourself some beautiful freshly cut flowers and place them in any room in your home that pleases you. If you're stuck indoors much of the time, for a change of pace consider spending some time outside. Have lunch at a café that has a garden or lush patio. Afterwards, order a coffee and read a book. Or, go for a walk in a park, or on a picnic with a friend. Mellow activities such as this will be helpful at de-stressing you. And a natural, calming environment will help you to get your bearings back.

Walk Around Your Neighborhood – You Might Find Some Hidden Treasures

If you live in a big city, chances are that there are interesting activities going on in your neighborhood that you probably don't even know about. You don't have to drive a far distance to become more social or at least, find a new favorite hangout to take your mind off your troubles. There might be a wonderful restaurant or coffeehouse close by that you've driven past but never entered, or a gym class offered where you can befriend your neighbors and get in shape at the same time. Instead of ignoring the world right outside your doorstep, take a walk and get to know your area. Walk into every store, check out every menu, talk to salespeople and baristas, take the time to sit in a coffeehouse, and strike up conversations with the people around you. It's important to have face-time with other people because living life online without deeper human interaction will make you feel lonelier and lengthen the time it takes for you to pull out of your depression.

Take a Trip

A weekend away at a hotel or bed and breakfast is a great way to clear your mind. If you have more time and money at your disposal, taking a week trip or longer is a terrific refresher. It's best to go with a friend so that you don't get lonely. Try some new cuisine at the restaurants and enjoy the local culture. Get involved in activities and be adventurous. Take lots of photos – these can become brand-new memories that have no association with your ex.

Breakup Survival Summaries

- If you have saved mementos from your relationship, either toss these items in the trash, or store them in a garbage or grocery bag until you're ready to decide what to do with them.
- Make changes to your living space so that you are not haunted by memories.
- Delete all photos of him stored in your cellphone and on your computer.
- Take things slow for a while as you adapt to your new life without your ex.
- Beautify your home and lift your mood by buying yourself beautiful flowers. Spend time outdoors and get some fresh air if you're stuck indoors most of the day.
- Find a place in your neighborhood to go that will help you get your mind off your difficulties, and allow you to be more social immediately.
- Take a weekend trip or longer with a friend so that you can create new memories that are not tied to your ex.

Chapter Three

Friends + Time = Recovery

The most important thing when recovering from a breakup is not to be isolated. Hiding away in your home and avoiding people will only make things worse, and lead to a longer, more difficult recovery. Sadness and depression can have a psychosomatic effect, causing you to feel anxious and tired. But being honest and open with good friends is the right medicine. Sharing your feelings will help you both mentally and physically. Because women tend to naturally develop support systems and are open with friends about their feelings, they often have an easier time recovering from a breakup than men, although this is not always the case.

At this time, avoid being around people who tend to be judgmental or competitive, or spend less time with them. When you're feeling better and regain your confidence you can bring them back into your life.

Being Discreet in a Work Environment

It's not easy showing a happy face and being productive when your heart has just been shattered. And you can't always carry on like a trooper. If co-workers begin to suspect that there is something amiss, or you feel the need to open up to someone at work, pick one person to speak with who is discreet and trustworthy. When you get your bearings back you can thank this person for their friendship and support by taking him or her to lunch, or buying them an appropriate gift.

Breaking Free from Depression

Not everyone has family or close friends who they feel comfortable confiding in. Some people have a support system, but it isn't enough; they need more help. Seeing a therapist is an option if you feel depressed for an extended period and believe that you're not pulling out of it. If you make the decision to see someone, it can remain a private decision that no one else need ever know about. If you choose to go this route, discuss your options with your health insurer or health service provider. If you aren't covered or the therapist you want to see is in private practice, ask them if they offer a sliding scale payment option to their patients who have difficulty affording regular counseling if this is an issue for you.

It's not unusual for someone to experience extreme emotional trauma after a breakup. Oftentimes, a breakup adds to the number of problems already present in a person's life. This combination of woes pushes them into deeper despair. In rare instances, some individuals contemplate ending their pain in the worst way imaginable. If you feel severely depressed at a particular moment and need to speak with someone immediately, you can. There are organizations located in most countries that are there to help. Some well-known centers are:

- The U.S. National Suicide Prevention Lifeline – (800) 273-8255
- The National Hopeline Network – (800) 442-4673
- Samaritins USA has 400 centers in 38 countries – (877) 870-4673
- Befrienders Worldwide – a global organization.
- Most popular messaging apps and social networks now have suicide prevention tools.

What is most important is that you get your perspective back. Your heartbreak and difficulties will eventually pass, although when you're going through it all you can't always see that clearly. No one is immune to the ups and downs of life. Being able to appreciate the simple things is important. There are so many things worth waking up to every morning, and they matter a great deal.

Be Kind to Yourself

- Try to keep daily stress to a minimum.
- Make sure that you exercise and look after your overall health.

- Get plenty of sleep.
- If you have many things to do on a day where you feel extremely down, do your errands and tasks slowly or break them up over several days if they aren't urgent.

After a breakup, it's not unusual for a person to lose confidence in their ability to meet someone new and feel that they are somehow not desirable enough for whatever reason to attract someone they would deem desirable. This is not the case in reality, yet it makes people feel hopeless and depressed for periods of time unnecessarily. Most of us have to go through some difficulties before meeting the right person. You might not have met this person yet, but you will eventually, so try to remain positive and patient.

Getting Your Sleep

Anxiety caused by a breakup can lead to sleep deprivation. Luckily, there are natural, healthy ways to cope and get your eight hours.

- Respect your body's need for rest and concentrate on pleasant thoughts before bedtime.
- Have a workout whenever possible, except for late at night – this will help you sleep. A brisk forty-minute walk or run around your area is a great way to get in a day's exercise.
- Avoid eating a heavy meal late at night and wait at least two hours before going to bed after eating.
- Drink a cup of warm milk or herbal tea in the

evening. Health food stores sell a variety of teas that can be helpful at relaxing you and reducing anxiety such as chamomile, valerian root, and passionflower. These are safe to drink for short periods of time unless you are allergic to one of the herbs listed. Remember to always check labels carefully.

- Avoid caffeinated beverages such as coffee, black tea, or soda late at night.

- If you awaken easily, consider wearing earplugs so that you can get uninterrupted sleep.

- Try to go to bed at the same time every evening so that your body adjusts and knows when to sleep.

- Make sure that the temperature in your bedroom is not too warm and that the lighting is comfortable for you. Some people prefer to go to sleep and wake up in a dark room, while others choose to allow sunlight entering their room in the morning to gently awaken them.

- If a particular scent or spice relaxes you, incorporate it into your evening meal or keep it by your bedside. The smell of coconuts might remind you of a trip you took to the tropics, or cinnamon might make you think of a cup of spiced cider during the holidays. Allow these wonderful scents to lull you into a relaxed state of mind.

- Reading can help you gradually fall asleep. A good book can take you to a faraway place and get your mind off your troubles.

Breakup Survival
Summaries

- Avoid being isolated.
- Share your feelings with caring and supportive people.
- Seeing a therapist is an option if you don't have a strong enough support system or feel that you are unable to pull yourself out of depression.
- Treat yourself in a gentle manner and look after your overall health.
- Make sure that you get your sleep. A good workout during the day or early evening will have a beneficial effect on your body and mind and help you sleep. Reading a good book at bedtime is also helpful.

Chapter Four

The Grieving Process

The earlier you allow yourself to grieve the end of your relationship the sooner you'll begin to feel better. Sometimes, friends and family who are trying to help, but don't always understand the circumstances or full extent of the hurt will suggest that you simply, "Get over it." Their intentions are well-meaning, but they are not the ones who are suffering. You can't just magically heal even though you wish you could. You have to go through the grieving process and there's no shortcut or overnight cure. Even if you're a strong and upbeat person it could take months for you to fully regain your emotional strength. Someone who has experienced a loss such as the death of a close friend or loved one, or has had several failed relationships, often recovers more quickly than a young person or a person who has experienced little loss in their life because they are more practiced at dealing with grief.

You will likely feel several different emotions, sometimes all within the same day for many weeks after the breakup. But it's not all bad news because you can find constructive ways to cope with them.

Disbelief and Denial

It's difficult to accept the finality of a breakup. The first wave of shock comes over you – you can't get your mind around the fact that it's really over. You are used to him being a part of your life and can't fathom him not being there. Some time goes by and you wonder whether he will come back or not. If he makes no attempt to reconcile, the second shock wave hits you and panic sets in. You wonder: Should I do something? Should I contact him? You begin to rationalize, trying to make sense of your situation. Sometimes people set time limits on reconciliation as if there were some sort of statute of limitations on making up. You might set some ground rules and tell yourself: If he calls within a week, I'll take him back. If he calls within a month, I won't. Then, the third and strongest wave hits – denial. You might think: He'll come back. This isn't happening. He loves me, I know it. This is only temporary.

The state of denial is the first major hurdle. Getting past this confusing time isn't easy. However, there are ways to adjust to this new reality: Don't set time limits for him or yourself regarding reconciliation. Don't try and convince yourself that he does or doesn't love you. Don't harp on the word *love*. Drop it from your vocabulary for now. Use your activities list and continually come up with ideas to keep yourself occupied.

Intense Longing

You long to be with him; you miss the sound of his voice, his scent, his touch. Memories become intensified and emotions run high. You wonder if you will ever feel such feelings again. Holding onto these moments becomes important. If you let them go, you are letting go a part of yourself. But then, you relive the anger and disappointment, and this outweighs the good memories. It's like a roller coaster ride that doesn't stop.

You can gain control of these feelings, but only if you put them into perspective. Consider the longing for him as normal, like the withdrawal someone experiences after ridding themselves of an addiction. When someone wants to lose weight, they can't continue eating junk food. When someone wants to stop smoking, they must stay away from cigarettes. If you want to quit your ex it's best to avoid seeing him, speaking with him, or even hearing about him. Go cold turkey.

Anger

Anger is a stage in the healing process that allows you to get stress out of your system. There is no shortage of ways in which to express it. Tearing up a shirt he used to wear that he left behind at your house, beating a pillow, or even making a voodoo doll and sticking pins in it are a few ways to do so. But these are only momentary releases. It's important that you have a way of dealing with anger that's productive and will have a positive effect on your life. My friend Casey is a good example of someone who was able to get past her angry stage in a healthy way.

As a twenty-six-year-old law student, Casey was under a great deal of pressure. All the loans she had taken out to pay for her education only added to her stress level. When Daniel, a twenty-eight-year-old student attending the same school cheated on her during their relationship, she felt like a boulder had been dropped on her. Daniel had been a close friend to her during their first year of school, and by the second year they had become intimate. When she found out through other students that he had been dating a woman in his Wills and Trusts class behind her back she was heartbroken and angry. She confronted Daniel between classes to find out the truth. He told her that the gossip going around was exaggerated. However, he admitted to dating the other woman. Casey was livid, but remained outwardly calm. "Did you really think that you could have a relationship with two women at the same school? Couldn't you have at least been smart enough to cheat on me with someone I don't know?" she said. Daniel struggled to defend himself in vain against the indefensible. Eventually, he gave up and told her that she had every right to be upset. Casey informed him bluntly, "We're through."

Although it was difficult seeing him every day while struggling to get through tough classes, Casey decided that she wasn't going to let the breakup with Daniel affect her grades or jeopardize her long-term goals. She realized that in law school she was living in a microcosm. After she passed her exams and graduated she would have better opportunities to socialize and date.

Casey had been taking a cycling class at the gym every Saturday afternoon to keep fit. Although she didn't have much spare time to exercise, she decided to sign up for another type of class as well: self defense. Every Tuesday night she took out the anger she felt towards Daniel on her opponents who were happy to take her on. School kept her mind occupied, and cycling and self defense classes kept her body fit and raised her spirits.

Anxiety

The end of your relationship technically puts you back where you started before you met him – square one. Because you no longer have someone special in your life, you long to fill that void. Some days you feel like you're in a mad rush to meet someone new. On other days you just want to be left alone and the thought of dating seems daunting.

You have control over many aspects of your life. If you work hard, you have a good chance of being successful. If you study, you will likely earn high marks in school. Dating is a completely different story because relationships are never a sure thing. Breakups cause a great deal of frustration and self-deprecation which can lead to lower self-confidence. Instead of denigrating yourself, continue doing stress relieving activities from your list and drawing support from close friends.

Feeling Blue

When feelings of sadness overtake you, cry when you feel like crying. Listen to songs that remind you of him and release your emotions. Soon you will tire of shedding tears and begin to adjust. Sometimes depression causes a person to feel tired and slow. If you're having a hard time functioning because you're grieving, go ahead and take a day off from work or leave early. But try not to do this more than once or twice. Your job is important - don't allow the breakup to have such an effect on you that you lose your livelihood.

Regret

You tell yourself: I wish I had done this or that differently. The shoulda-woulda-coulda trap can keep you up nights. You can't go back in time and undue what occurred and neither can he. Replaying the same scenes in your head and rewriting them like a movie script the way you wish they had played out is pointless. It keeps you living in the past which you can't change.

The one good thing that comes out of regret is that it teaches you about yourself. If you believe that you made a serious mistake, own up to it and accept responsibility, and then make the decision not to make the same error in your *next* relationship. Once you come to your conclusions and make that promise to yourself, don't harp on it anymore.

You Begin to Snap Out of Your Sadness

You are tired of being depressed. Your mind and body both want you to pull out of it and are telling you so. Your appetite is back, if it was ever gone - some people never lose their appetite. Your interest in your appearance returns, and you're brushing your hair regularly and applying your makeup with care. You're thinking about buying new clothes, and you're interested in being stylish and looking pretty again. You want to do something fun and interesting. You feel like being around people and talking about subjects other than him. You want to rejoin the world and feel alive again.

Breakup Survival Summaries

- Allow yourself time to grieve. Don't try and skip this process or rush yourself through it because doing so will slow down your recovery in the long-term.
- Denial, longing, anger, anxiety, sadness, and regret are some of the many feelings you will experience. Let them play out and find constructive ways to deal with them.
- Eventually, you will reach the point where you don't want to feel down anymore. Your mind and body will come to a consensus and you'll want to rejoin the world.

Chapter Five

Staying Strong

Don't Let Curiosity Get the Best of You

Where is he going? What is he doing? Who is he with? These are questions that can eat at you non-stop. The temptation to drive by his home or workplace in hopes of catching a glimpse of him can be overwhelming. The mystery of not knowing about what's happening in his life makes him seem unobtainable and desirable. Because you can't contact him and simply ask him what he's been up to, you invent all sorts of scenarios in your mind. You think to yourself: Maybe he's already found someone else. You imagine he's out every night meeting other women. Or, you are concerned that other women are coming across his profile somewhere online or on dating sites, finding him attractive, and contacting him. An overactive imagination and directing your energy towards this frame of thought is counterproductive. And driving by his apartment or workplace to see if his car is there or the lights are on doesn't give you much information about what's going on with him. In actuality, things are probably pretty much the same. The only difference is that you're no longer in his life.

You Accidentally Run into One of His Close Friends

One of the most awkward and dreaded situations is crossing paths with an ex's close friend in person or online. The first thought is almost always to duck and run, but then other ideas pop up and you consider your options. You might think: Should I just say hello like a normal person? If I pretend that I didn't notice him would it look natural? Could I get away with subtly questioning him to find out if my ex is seeing someone?

Remember that this person is your ex's friend, not yours, and he will do and say what he feels is in the best interest of his friend. There's no harm in saying a polite hello and asking him what he's been up to lately. You can also share some basics about what's been going on in your life. But avoid going into the whole spiel and keep your cards to yourself. If he volunteers information about your ex, then so be it. But don't delve further or prompt him for more details – it's not healthy to go on a fishing expedition. If you dig too deep, you might find out something that hits a nerve. Avoid having your buttons pushed, and in this instance, protect yourself *from* yourself.

Try Some New Hangouts

You don't have to stop going to your favorite restaurant or pub because there is a possibility of running into your ex if you were regulars as a couple. But it's probably a good idea to stop by at an hour when you know he's least likely to be there, at least until you're in a stronger place emotionally. Now is a great time to try some new places where you don't have memories trailing you.

Don't Search Online for Information About Him

It's not uncommon for someone recovering from a breakup to become curious about what their ex is doing. To alleviate this, they will search for information about them online – the most obvious place to look is at their social media accounts, if they have any. If they see that their ex's relationship status has changed or a photo of him with a new woman, they will then check her profile page to find out more about her. But connecting the dots can be challenging and on some of these sites an obvious trail is left behind. If this describes what you've been doing, break the pattern and stop tormenting yourself. Using social media for this activity is mentally taxing and checking these accounts can lead to an unhealthy obsession, keeping you from moving forward with your life.

Keep in mind that no one's life is frozen in time – things happen to people constantly such as career changes, marriages, divorces, weddings, funerals, and travel. You are no longer in his life and he is no longer in yours, so none of the people displayed in the photographs on his profile page should be of relevance to you. Watching his life unfold as an outsider is pointless and a complete waste of your time. Instead, spend your time creating a better life for yourself and leave him in the past where he belongs.

Messaging Apps and Your Ex

The only way that you can see your ex's profile photo on a messaging app or when he last used the app is if you keep his number in your cellphone. His "last seen" or "last online" status doesn't really tell you anything about his life, only when he last used the app. If his "last seen" was at 3 a.m., it doesn't necessarily mean that he stayed out all night with a new love interest. It might mean that he sent a message to his mother overseas who lives in a different time zone. This is why it's imperative that you remove his number from your phone.

How to Handle a Situation Where Your Ex Has a Publicist

If your ex works for a high-profile company, is a well-known person, or a member of an affluent family, you might come across information about him online that pops up unexpectedly. Stories about VIP's and their family members are spun by public relations machines, so don't believe the spin. Everyone at some point suffers trauma and setbacks in their lives, but a good publicist is skilled at keeping those details hidden. What is written for public consumption is often sheer fabrication. You might read that your ex is now dating a gorgeous model. However, in reality she hardly knows him and just happened to be standing next to him in a photo for a fundraiser. And even if they did end up dating and getting married, few celebrity marriages last very long. There's no point in making yourself upset over something that either isn't true or won't stand the test of time, so avoid the temptation to read these articles.

Don't Try to Be His Friend

When you're vulnerable and hurt, it makes no sense to hold on to the source of pain. Your life might feel empty without him while you're adjusting, but attempting to fill that void by turning your ex into a friend will only slow your progress in getting over him. Even worse, it keeps you living in the past. It also gives you the horrible feeling of being demoted. If you have a strong desire to hold on to him as a friend, ask yourself if your true motive is to get close to him so that you can win him back. If he began dating other women and chose to discuss those relationships with you, would it get under your skin? Be honest with yourself – most likely it would. When you are no longer emotionally invested in him, you might choose to be his friend. Until that time, it's foolish to think that being his pal will have a positive influence on your life.

41

Are You Flirting with the Idea of Getting Back Together with Him...for All the Wrong Reasons?

Our lives are multi-dimensional. We have our careers, we socialize with friends and family, and we have romantic relationships. When one aspect of our life falters, it's only natural to try and offset that loss by directing our attention towards other things that are going well. For example: If you dislike your job but you have someone to come home to who you have a secure and loving relationship with, the enjoyment of your job on a daily basis is less vital to your well-being. Whereas, if your relationship ends, but you have a job that is rewarding and a group of supportive friends whose company you enjoy, it will be easier for you to accept a romantic loss.

If you're feeling lonely and as if things haven't been going your way lately, it's probably a good time to make some changes. If your job isn't leading you in the direction you want, consider getting into a field that you find more interesting. Join clubs, network with colleagues, and socialize more in order to make new friends if your old ones are too busy to spend time with you or have drifted away. By improving other areas of your life and setting your sights on your goals, the breakup will hold less significance.

Believe It or Not, Having to Pay Your Bills Is a Godsend

The first concern of most people is to keep a roof over their heads, as well as put food on the table, and pay their bills. At any point in life this can mean working extra hours, taking on another job, starting a business, or going back to school. When most of your time is taken up with concerns of survival, you can't sit around thinking about your ex. You have to plot out a strategy to remain competitive and reposition yourself in preparation for changes up ahead. The grit of life is enough to tear you down. However, after a major disappointment it can be your saving grace. Time really does the trick. The harder you work and the more responsibilities you have, the quicker it flies. One day, many years from now, you may come to view your past in blocks of time. You'll remember that you once worked for a certain company, and at that time you were dating so-and-so, and the relationship ended.

Always remember to count your blessings. There are things you have that others don't, be it your good health, a caring family, a good job, or enough money in the bank. If you're grateful for what you *do* have you won't pay so much attention to what you don't.

The Wisdom of Strangers

If you think you've been having a rough time lately, think again. When you open up to strangers, you'll find that you're not alone. Personal dramas you'll hear from ordinary folks will blow you away. These conversations can take place online, or you might be on a plane for a few hours and get seated next to a friendly, talkative person. Or, maybe you'll end up sitting on the subway next to someone for a long ride. Try striking up a conversation once in awhile. If you open up first, that person might share their experiences too. It's often helpful to get the opinion of someone who is a complete outsider. They might have some good advice and a different take on life.

Breakup Survival Summaries

- Don't waste your time and energy checking on your ex's comings and goings from his home or workplace.
- If you run into one of his friends, simply be polite. If he volunteers information about your ex, that's his prerogative. Although it might be tempting, avoid wheedling information out of him.
- If you have a favorite restaurant or hangout and your ex likes going there too, you should still go and enjoy yourself. But consider going at an hour when it's unlikely he'll drop by until you're over him. You should also scout out new places.
- Don't look up your ex online to see what he's been up to lately. Doing this can lead to an unhealthy obsession.
- Make sure that you've deleted his number from your cellphone so that you aren't tempted to check his "last seen" status on an app that you know he uses. This information will only tell you that he is using the app regularly. It will not give you an accurate depiction of what's happening in his life.
- Don't try to be your ex's friend. It will keep you from fully getting over him because he will still have a role in your life.
- You can have a full life with or without being in a relationship by having a career you find satisfying and friends whose company you enjoy.
- Most of us have to work hard to get by every day. The more responsibilities you have, the quicker

time flies. And as time passes, the hurt goes away too.

- If you think that life has been tough lately, try opening up to strangers. It's likely their stories will be even more harrowing than yours. Sharing your experiences with a complete outsider will give you a fresh perspective.

Chapter Six

Avoid Comparing Your Life to the Lives of Others

When you walk around town after a breakup, couples seem to stand out more. You never paid much attention to them before, but now, suddenly they're everywhere. You feel a visceral response when you see them holding hands and looking blissful – you're alone, and these people have someone. Try not to see the world as a place where you lose, and others win. What you see when you look at a couple is a picture frozen in time. They appear to be happy at that moment, and they are together on that day. Whether or not they remain a couple is an unwritten story, and unless you know them personally you'll never know the ending. And although misery loves company, in your heart you probably wish them well.

Looking at the social media pages of others can have an even worse effect on a person's psyche because people use these sites to promote themselves or entertain an audience. What you see on social media is not a genuine portrayal of a person's life. They are displaying a sugar-coated version, and sometimes what's posted is completely fake. When someone is skilled at self-promotion, they can make others believe that they have it all when they don't. So, don't ever compare yourself to these fraudsters, and don't let the narcissistic tendencies of others affect how you feel about yourself. Detoxing from social media and cutting yourself off from all the nonsense is often the best thing to do.

It's best at all times, not just while recovering from a breakup, to avoid comparing your life to the lives of others. It's easy to envy people who you believe have a better life and what appears to be a good relationship. However, since you're on the outside looking in, you really don't know whether the person you envy or admire is happy, or has the life that they want. You don't know what's going on in another person's mind or how they view their current situation. The person you envy might secretly envy you. There are plenty of people who are disillusioned and disappointed in their relationships. People can feel lonely even surrounded by a large circle of family and friends. No one can predict what will happen in the future. The unexpected always pops up in people's lives, be it good or bad. Complete reversals of fortune are commonplace in this world. Look upon this time when you find yourself single again as a period in which you have the opportunity to do things you wouldn't be able to do if you were in a serious relationship. And remember, although you might be feeling lonely now because of the breakup, these feelings and your current situation will not last forever.

A positive way to view the lack of romance in your life at any given time is to tell yourself that you would like to have romantic love, but that you don't need it to feel complete. Romantic love will come again when you're in a good state of mind and are open to it. You can't always force it to come when you want it unfortunately, but with or without it you can enjoy life. There are other forms of love too – they might not be the romantic kind, but they are also wonderful; the love you give and receive from close friends and family, the passion for a career you've chosen, and the love for a sport or hobby you're good at. Life is not empty without romance, not by a long-shot.

When the Feelings Are Right but the Timing Is Off

All over the world, millions of men and women meet each other every day and begin dating. But personal issues and outside pressures influence each person's openness to commitment. People's needs and desires change constantly, and when a couple succeeds it has a lot to do with a meeting of the minds. Sometimes two people are right for each other, but the timing is off. There are all sorts of things that can happen in a person's life to make them unavailable for a relationship. It can be personal or financial difficulties, family or work pressures, a desire to reach their goals, or a lack of maturity, meaning that the person doesn't know himself well enough to know what he wants in life. The tragedy of bad timing is that there's nothing you can do about it. The only way to handle the situation is to go on with your life - date other men and put the relationship behind you. It's possible that if you and your ex had met at a different time in your lives the relationship would have had a better chance of survival due to any number of reasons. So, if you feel it's applicable, you can place some of the blame on timing.

Oftentimes, the fact that a relationship fails is a blessing and it's for the best in the long-run that it ended. You'll look back later in life and realize how lucky you were that you had the time to travel, start a new career, or meet the *real* love of your life. When you meet the right person, you'll know it and so will he. This man won't allow outside pressures to get in the way of being with you, and the timing will be right.

Respect Yourself and Everything Else Falls into Place

When you feel happy in your own skin, you are never lonely. You have friends, hobbies, and interests that keep you busy and satisfied. Having a man in your life is fantastic, but not having one can be great too. A woman who feels empty without a man will often find herself in unsatisfying relationships because she clings to whoever is in her life, even if she knows things are not working or is unhappy. If you think that you might have a problem in this regard, there are steps you can take to turn it around:

- Think of all the fun activities you can do alone. This could be watching your favorite films, listening to music, jogging, shopping, crafts, having coffee and a pastry in the morning while reading the news, doing yoga, pilates, or any number of things. Also, think of a hobby you might enjoy or an interest you haven't spent time cultivating because you directed all your energy towards finding or keeping a man in your life, and pursue it.

- Realize that being single is okay. People find themselves single for all sorts of reasons and this can happen at any stage of life. Being single is not a *bad* thing and being alone doesn't mean that you have to be lonely.

Miss Independence

The polar opposite of being needy, being so independent that you give men no opportunity to be chivalrous and romance you can also be disastrous to your dating life. Women who are self-assured and display a great deal of confidence sometimes appear closed.

If you are moving into a new building and have handled most of the moving and unpacking yourself, if an attractive gentleman in the building offers to help you with the last bits, allow him to if you find him interesting. Don't tell him: "I've already done most of it myself. Thank you, but it's not necessary." If your attitude is always, "I can do it myself," you will find yourself alone. Don't look at accepting advice or help from men as being a damsel in distress. Let them be kind and enjoy the attention.

What to do if You Find Out That Your Ex Has Moved on Quickly

You can't believe the news when you hear through the grapevine that your ex has moved in with another woman shortly after your relationship ended. To you this is the ultimate betrayal and a shock to your system. You get the horrible feeling that you've been erased overnight and all the time and effort you put into the relationship has already been wiped out. Not only is he gone completely from your life, but he is in bed with someone else. He sees this woman every day, spends time with her, and is living a new life. You think to yourself: Did he feel absolutely nothing for me? Doesn't he miss me or think about me at all? How could he have become so serious with someone he just met? Is he on the rebound? Will his new relationship last?

When a man moves on quickly after a breakup it is often due to loneliness or the fact that he has no one in his life who he can confide in. Unlike women, men tend not to maintain a support system made up of friends that they can share their feelings with. A man relies on the woman in his life to listen and be there for him. In all likelihood, if he's moved on right away after the breakup, it's because he craves closeness to another person. When a man is in this state of mind he might become involved with someone he finds appealing in some ways, but is probably not his ideal partner. If a man has the strength to get past his loneliness and give himself time to date, he has a greater chance of meeting someone who has more of the traits that he finds desirable. When he rushes into something, he's likely to realize later that he made a mistake. This is why these types of relationships are referred to as "rebounds". The one thing to keep in mind however, is this: Once a couple is already together they can negotiate and come to terms on important issues. If the woman he's living with is willing to make whatever changes he requests to please him, she might be able to maintain his interest in the long-term.

Few people are able to jump right back into dating after a breakup; most need time to heal and grieve. If your ex didn't allow himself this time and jumped right into something new, he will probably have a delayed reaction and feel the full intensity of his loss several months or even years from now. But that's not your problem. Your relationship is over and whether he's living alone or with another woman is not your concern. Consider this: It's doubtful that the woman he is involved with is his dreamgirl, so remove all the worst-case-scenarios from your head. Avoid looking her up on social media or checking his profile page for signs of her. He is in your past now, so leave him there.

Breakup Survival
Summaries

- When you envy or admire someone, you are on the outside looking in. That person might not feel lucky and fulfilled in their life. In fact, they might feel that you have it better than they do.
- A lot of what people post on social media is exaggerated or even fake. Don't let other people's need to pretend that they are on top of the world, when most likely they aren't, affect your psychological state. Don't waste your time comparing yourself to these people because most of the time you will be comparing yourself to a bogus creation.
- Sometimes the success or failure of a relationship has a lot to do with timing. If you feel that bad timing played a role in your breakup, there's nothing you can do about it now. Accept that it was a contributing factor, and move on.
- Learn to be comfortable in your own skin whether you're single or in a relationship.
- If you find out that your ex has moved on quickly, it might shock you at first. But don't concern yourself with what he's doing or who he is involved with because it no longer matters. Look towards the future and leave him in the past.

Chapter Seven

Reward Yourself - You Deserve It

It's not easy letting someone you love go, let alone someone who you were close to on a physical level. After some time has gone by, the gray fog around you will lift a little bit at a time. While this is happening, do whatever is necessary to cheer yourself up. Ask yourself this question: What are the things that make me happy under normal circumstances?

Have you been daydreaming about signing up for dance class, or spending a day at the beach? Don't daydream about it, do it. If you think that dining out will lift your spirits, go to your favorite restaurant with a friend and order a dish that you love. If you think that shopping might help, buy yourself some beautiful things that you've had your eye on for a while. You deserve a reward for the strength you've shown. Treating yourself should give you a strong kick in a more positive direction.

Food Glorious Food!

It's important to eat right and stay healthy, even when you want to gorge on ice cream and chocolates in an attempt to self-medicate yourself out of depression. It's generally not a good idea to use food as a pick-me-up because it can become habit. But after a devastating breakup, you can cut yourself some slack. It's not breaking your diet if you treat yourself to two decadent meals a week; doing this gives you a guilty pleasure to look forward to that will temporarily relieve stress and anxiety. But only allow yourself this treat if you have a strong craving for a rich meal. Don't do it for the heck of it. The idea is to give yourself some leeway during a down period in your life, not overeat and make yourself ill (nausea would defeat the purpose), or pack on pounds. Set a time limit so that you don't gain weight – for most people two or three weeks is reasonable. You might choose to be mindful of your health by using substitutes. Instead of having a dinner of steak and potatoes, and a slice of cake for dessert, have salmon and vegetables, and fruit for dessert with a bit of chocolate sauce drizzled on top. A dinner combination such as this is a satisfying alternative.

Alcohol should never be used as a panacea. Since you're still recovering, don't drink until you are well beyond the grieving stage and are feeling like your normal self again. When you reach that point, you can go out with your friends to celebrate the fact that you're over your ex with a few glasses of champagne.

Go Shopping!

Now is a great time to assess your wardrobe. Doing this will give you an in-house project to help you keep your mind off your ex. Set aside clothes that you never wear and put them in a pile. These can be sold online, or you can drop them off at a thrift shop or local charity. Getting rid of old or unworn clothes clears clutter, and selling or giving certain items away allows you to shed memories of the recent past.

After you've gotten rid of your unwanted clothing, buy yourself some new things that you feel you need or have always wanted. Buy clothes that are cut well, look great on you, and suit your true personality. Plus, throw in a sexy number and start wearing it immediately. Getting male attention after a breakup is a terrific ego booster.

You might also consider stocking up on some lingerie. Purchase that sexy little chemise you've had your eye on for weeks but figured you wouldn't need after the breakup. Hopefully, you'll be wearing it soon. Being optimistic about meeting someone new is smart, but being ready is even smarter.

Get a Makeover

It's always a definite plus when you're confident and know what looks great on you in regard to makeup. If you're not someone who is entirely secure in this department, maybe it's time to think about what you can do to look your most beautiful and current. There's no need to make drastic changes. Some small additions to your makeup bag will do the trick, or possibly removing an old favorite that has become passé. Most of us have gone through a stage in life when we've become overly attached to a certain item, leaving us in a makeup time-warp. Having an updated look is important because being current is youthful and in-the-know. A change can be as simple as buying a shade of blush that gives you a natural-looking healthy glow, a makeup base containing the latest skin-enhancing technology, or adding extra pop to your eyes with a new shade of eyeshadow. The great thing about makeup is that you don't need to spend a lot of money to get that added bit of glamour, and one small purchase can last for months. So, maybe it's time to head over to your favorite beauty supply shop to check out the latest arrivals. Sometimes looks that begin as trends end up lasting years. Why not be on the cutting edge?

If you feel that you'd like a bigger change than just new makeup, you might consider a different haircut or color that you think would better flatter your face-shape and complexion. If you're not up to trying out an all-over color, subtle highlights can have the same effect but without the shock factor. Or, buy some extensions and add some length to your locks.

Visit a Day Spa

Allowing yourself to be pampered for a day in a calming, restorative environment might be just what you need. Stop into an elegant spa and check out their list of services. If the prices are over the top and you think it would be a financial stretch, try another. Ask your friends for their advice; they might be able to give you the scoop on which spas offer the best services.

Arrive well in advance of your appointment and have a cup of tea, if offered. Enjoy a massage, plus whichever treatments you think will relax you. A day at the spa can be incredibly rejuvenating. You might even walk out feeling like you've just returned from a week's vacation. Consider how expensive that would have been. You'll have saved yourself a lot of money.

Try a Treatment Bath

Sophisticated versions of the time-tested bubble-bath are a way to enjoy a spa-like experience at home. If you love the smell of a particular flower, buy it in an essential oil and add it to your bath. Light some floral-scented candles, and even throw in petals. Finish off your soak with scented body lotion. An elegant bath pillow or an in-bath body massager is a great addition. A long, warm bath will soothe your aching muscles, relax your body, and raise your spirits.

Exercise

Exercise is a great anti-depressant - the key to enjoying it is to avoid boredom. Try a variety of exercises that work out different muscle groups or sign up for a class that interests you. Lift some weights to obtain a firm physique and strengthen your bones, or use exercise bands.

If gyms and exercise classes don't interest you, a brisk walk can work wonders too. Power-walking is an effective cardio workout. If the area around your home is unsuitable for walks due to traffic or a lack of scenery, drive over to a place that's better for that activity. If there's a part of town you've always dreamt of living, you can take your walks there. Bring a friend and you can both get some fresh air and exercise.

Keeping It Real

Before you make your appointments and decide on purchases, assess what you can and can't afford. There's nothing wrong with buying on a whim, but be reasonable. Enjoy yourself, but don't ignore the voice in your head that tells you when you've gone too far

Quiz

How do you think your recovery is going so far? Have you had a set-back and contacted your ex? Has rewarding yourself actually made you feel better? Answering these questions will help you assess whether or not you're on the right track. Circle your answers and tally up your score:

1. When you got the urge to contact your ex recently, how did you handle it?

a. I gave him a call because I needed to speak with him so that I could get my stuff back and clear some issues.

b. I sent him a chat message and asked him how he was doing.
c. I added his number back into my phone and spied on him through messaging apps.
d. I exercised and then called a friend.

2. When you were sitting at home alone in front of your computer the other day and he popped into your mind, what did you do?

a. I checked his social media page using a fake account.
b. I searched several dating sites, checking to see if he was a member.
c. I composed a chat message but decided not to send it.
d. I concentrated on what I was doing and put him out of my mind.

3. If you saw your ex's mother at the grocery store what would your reaction be?

a. I would pull her aside and attempt to wheedle information out of her about her son.
b. I would suddenly become nervous and leave the store.
c. I would duck behind the avocados and pray that she didn't see me.

d. I would acknowledge her with a polite hello if I crossed her path and then go about my shopping.

4. When members of your family who took a liking to your ex inquire about him, what is your response?

a. I'm not speaking with certain relatives at the moment because they keep talking about him.

b. I raise my voice and tell them, "Enough already!" and leave the family party early.

c. I tell them that I once deeply cared for him, but unfortunately, the relationship couldn't be salvaged.

d. I explain to my family that it's over and they should accept it.

5. When you came across a photo of him that somehow survived the purging process, what did you do with it?

a. I saved the photo on my cellphone.

b. I directed my attention elsewhere, but I didn't delete it.

c. I downloaded it onto a flash drive, placed it with my stash of "ex-stuff," and put it in a place where I wouldn't come across it.

d. I deleted it.

6. On days when you're feeling especially down about the breakup, what do you do?

a. I leave work early, go home, stuff myself with brownies, and cry.
b. I go to work and return home, but that's about it. I'm not ready to socialize or get back to my normal life.
c. I call a good friend and talk about how I'm feeling.
d. I finish my workday, have dinner, relax awhile, and then take a brisk walk. Afterwards, I watch a movie I've been looking forward to seeing.

7. On the days you've chosen to spoil yourself, what action do you take?

a. I decide that it's pointless. Nothing makes me feel better.
b. Although I've set aside some money, I haven't gotten around to treating myself because I've been too depressed.
c. The other day I spotted a dress that I wanted in a store window. I've walked past it many times, but haven't tried it on yet.
d. I've worked out a budget and treat myself when the urge takes me.

Let's See Your Score:

A's = 1 point
B's = 2 points
C's = 3 points
D's = 4 points

7-12 points:

You are still in the beginning stages of the grieving process, so go easy on yourself. Avoid being isolated and call your friends regularly. You might want to have a friend contact you at different intervals of the day to check up on you until you're feeling better. As you heal you will go through different stages of grief, and you'll lean on friends less and less as your recovery progresses.

13-18 points:

Getting over your ex is a struggle for you, but at the same time you are able to come to terms with the end of the relationship. Spend more time with supportive people and think of new activities that would be more effective at keeping you focused on things other than him. Make sure that they are right for you and that you will really do them.

19-23 points:

You have your confidence back, are functioning at full capacity, and are optimistic about the future. Some days are harder than others, but you're confident enough to handle the situation.

24-28 points:
Your recovery is coming along brilliantly. Whatever you're doing is working, so keep it up.

Breakup Survival Summaries

- You've suffered from feeling blue and fighting the temptation to contact your ex. Reward yourself for those accomplishments.
- Enjoy your favorite foods, buy some new clothes, spend a day at the spa, or do whatever you think will cheer you up. Make sure that you treat yourself, but only in ways that you can afford.
- Quiz yourself on your progress. If you're still in the early stages of grieving after several weeks have passed, spend more time with supportive friends. And also, think of new activities that will help you keep your mind off your ex.

Chapter Eight

How to Handle an Ex Who Is Still in Your Life

You See Your Ex Every Day at Work

The slow-developing romance that occurs between two people who work together, enjoy each other's company, and realize that they want to become involved romantically, often leads them to the altar. But when an office romance goes sour, it can make for an incredibly sticky situation. If you find yourself in this quandary and you're dreading going to work, keep your chin up – there are ways to deal with it. During the awkward stage immediately after your breakup there are a number of things you can do to make your situation more tenable:

1. Talk to him in a polite, respectful manner. Tell him that since your jobs and reputations are important to you both, you have no option but

to show a classy face to your co-workers and get along in public.

2. Anything that the two of you feel you need to talk about can be discussed after work and away from the office at a neutral location such as a coffeehouse, or over the phone on your own time. It's a good idea to keep these discussions face-to-face and not use messaging apps because sometimes people keep records. Conversations that take place through apps are often more casual than people realize and can give a bad impression to outsiders.

3. Never use company email to discuss private issues. Under certain circumstances these emails can be accessed if the company you work for chooses to view them.

4. Take on work assignments that he's not directly involved in if you have that option until things cool down.

Display Confidence at the Office

The most masterful way to handle an uncomfortable office situation is to simply do your work and avoid looking disheveled or distraught. Showing up on time every day and behaving in a professional manner sends a clear message that you are serious about your job. If you stand tall, exude confidence, and continue to prove your competence and interest in your work, co-workers will be less likely to take seriously any rumors that might be circulating.

If you and your ex are able to pull through this

situation unscathed and possibly even be comfortable working with each other again, you've truly accomplished something. The name of the game is to keep your job - and your sanity.

You See Your Ex on Campus

A college campus appears to be a massive, sprawling place at first. But when your ex attends the same school it suddenly feels a lot smaller. Is there a coffeehouse or hangout that you and your ex both regularly visited when you were dating? What would you do if you were to walk inside to get a cup of your usual blend and ran into him standing with a group of his friends? Here is a suggestion: Remain outwardly calm, even if your heart is pounding so hard that you think others can hear it. Nod your head in polite acknowledgment if your eyes meet. Order your coffee, and when it's ready, head out the door. You don't need to speak - your body language can speak for you. Send him the message that your world has not been shattered. Give him the vibe that you are busy with your studies and have to get to class or write a paper that's due soon. That's the purpose of going to school in the first place. Your ex knows this because he's working towards the same goals. Accepting the fact that you might bump into him once in awhile and that it can't be avoided will help you adjust. Relax – he's an ex-boyfriend. How many people on campus have an ex roaming around? I'd say the percentage has got to be pretty high. You're hardly alone.

You Run in the Same Social Circles

When a relationship ends, friends that you made as a couple are stuck in the middle. They have to think carefully about which one of you they are going to invite for dinner or join them for an event. Usually, people sympathize with the person who was mistreated and gravitate towards them. However, there are no assurances for the one who suffered most because a talented manipulator can sway the crowd in their favor. Oftentimes, after a divorce or a long-term relationship ends, people lose longtime friends causing them to feel abandoned. People who you were both close to might decide to stay away until things have calmed down, while others you might have to write off. Friends that you made as an individual, who had little or no contact with him will most likely remain loyal.

If you lose some friends after the breakup, there are many ways you can look at the situation, and believe it or not, not all angles are bad. One immediate benefit is that you can now pick and choose friends based solely on whose company *you* enjoy, and no longer consider what activities he liked, and whose company he preferred. During your relationship, you may have attended parties or regularly had dinner with people you didn't particularly care for. Well, lucky you – you don't have to see them anymore.

Most people categorize friends, although they might not be aware of it. There are those who you keep close to you as trusted confidantes, some are acquaintances who you see occasionally, while others are on the periphery of your life. The best way to handle a loss whether it's temporary or permanent is to do a reshuffling of friends and try to make new ones. If you'd like to do a reshuffling, here are some suggestions: The first thing you should do is reach out to the friends who you suspect are no longer going to be a part of your life because your assumptions about them might be incorrect. A couple that hasn't called you in a month may have gone on an extended vacation, lost a loved one close to them such as a parent, or simply wanted to take a break from socializing. You'll never know unless you contact them. Next, think of an individual who you've always liked but never spent time cultivating a friendship with because most of your time was taken up when you were in a relationship. This person may be either in the acquaintance category or even on the periphery of your life - it doesn't matter. Get in touch with them and suggest you meet for lunch, or take part in an event or sport. If they have the time and the activity you suggest piques their interest, they might decide to set aside a day to spend with you. That day could lead to a friendship that is healthier and more valuable than the ones you lost.

Breakup Survival
Summaries

- If you work in the same office as your ex, suggest being civil since you both value your jobs.
- If you have issues to discuss, this can be done after work at a neutral location or over the phone.
- Avoid using messaging apps when discussing your breakup. Viewed by others, these chats can paint a negative picture of your character that is inaccurate.
- Continue to prove your competence at work; don't let the breakup jar you.
- If you are a student and attending the same college as your ex, although it's tough, remember that the purpose of being at school is to attend classes and study so that you will have future opportunities in life. This should be your main focus.
- If you and your ex run in the same social circles you may lose friends after the breakup. This might be permanent or temporary. If you lose a friend or two don't obsess about getting them back. Instead, try to make new friends by socializing more and reacquainting yourself with the people you already know.

Chapter Nine

Achieving Closure

Closure happens when you believe that you know the fundamental reasons why the relationship ended, and you don't want or need to rehash what occurred. It is the equivalent of saying to yourself: "My relationship is over, and I know more or less why. And it no longer matters. It's time to let go and move on." But unfortunately, not everyone is able to do this. Sometimes, people ignore warning signs that things are going badly while in a relationship and remain in denial until the very end. This makes it harder for them to fully let go.

When a person is in love they look for the good in their partner and rationalize away negative behaviors. They are so busy looking for positive signs that they often miss the obvious. This is one of the main reasons that after a breakup, people are left feeling confused. If this represents you, you might consider doing an analysis of the relationship through a writing exercise. The main purpose of this exercise is for you to reach an epiphany that ends your confusion. You will no longer have unanswered questions haunting you. It's that moment when you say, "Aha! That's why things unfolded as they did. I now feel that I know all I need to know. I can finally let go."

Let's begin the closure process by looking at your ex's personality and behavior. Write down all the good things about his personality. What were the qualities that drew you to him and held your interest? What made him special or different from other men you've dated? What were the defining moments when you felt that he was the right person for you? This can be titled List #1. Underneath that paragraph or series of bullet points (however you choose to organize your thoughts), write what you didn't like about him in detail. Be honest in your evaluation. Don't give credit where it isn't due, and don't demonize him either - simply state your perspective. Remember, this list is solely for you. You won't be showing it to anyone else.

Pull up another blank page and title it List #2. Write down what you feel your ex did to improve your relationship and what he did to harm it. Under the "Improve the Relationship" category, some examples might be: He was supportive of your work and ambitions. Or, maybe you trusted him and never felt suspicious or wondered where he was; the relationship ended because of reasons other than infidelity. Under the "Harm the Relationship" category, two examples might be: He was inconsiderate of your feelings and belittled you. Or, he developed a flirtatious friendship with another woman, and you suspected him of cheating.

It takes two to build something together, but it takes one or several actions by one or both parties to irreparably damage it and bring it to an end. In a new paragraph, write what *you* did to make the relationship better, and what you did that was wrong. Underneath that, write down what the relationship dynamics were. Do you feel that the relationship was a healthy one? Were arguments resolved? Were either of you bored with the relationship or not put enough effort into it? If you were to compare your relationship to a musical piece, would you say that it was melodious or off-key?

Now, make a third list - List #3. Write down the clues that indicated something was seriously wrong and made you wonder if the relationship was salvageable. What were the definitive moments and series of events that occurred? Couples break up because they can't get past an issue – what was it? This list is the most important because it describes the downward spiral that led to the end of the relationship.

Once more, pull up another blank page and title it List #4. Write down how the relationship ended. Was it abrupt or drawn-out? Did you leave him because you were unhappy and had little optimism that things would get better? Did he walk out on you? Did he pull a disappearing act and cut off all communication? Write down what occurred that brought the relationship to its final end.

At the end of this writing exercise you should have a better understanding of yourself, your ex, and why the relationship ended. Hopefully, you will have an epiphany while making your lists, but if you don't have it now, it will come eventually. It might happen unexpectedly while you're driving or doing something you normally do every day. You'll come to important conclusions and say to yourself: "My confusion has ended!" You'll finally be able to connect the dots and mysteries will unfold automatically. Keep these four lists handy so that you will be able to find them should you feel the need to refer to them.

In addition to your lists you can help yourself further by recording your feelings and suspicions about what happened during your relationship privately throughout the day on your cellphone recorder. Some people even prefer making voice recordings over lists, although doing both is by far the most helpful. Playing them back to yourself when you find the time will aid you in reaching important conclusions.

Feel Good About Having Been Hopeful

Hope is what propels the human spirit. No invention would ever be discovered, and no one would venture out into the world if they didn't have hope. The fact that you invested so much of yourself in another person is a wonderful thing. You experienced the freedom of allowing someone to enter your world and share your life. Endings are always hard; the finality of it and the fact that the person is no longer available are both devastating. But you had this person in your life and enjoyed what he had to give and teach you. He also learned from you. You had shared experiences which you can draw lessons from. If you'd like, light a candle in honor of what the relationship meant to you, and to mark the end of it. Cherish the good memories. And most of all, be proud that you were hopeful.

Improving Your Self-Esteem After Rejection

All human beings experience rejection throughout their lives. No one has stellar luck and always wins – life doesn't work that way. Recovering from a romantic rejection is excruciatingly painful and can affect a person's self-esteem negatively, often for a long period of time. Working on your self-esteem will enable you to lessen the pain you experience during the healing process and will give you more self-insight so that you can regain your perspective. To begin this process, it's important to recognize when your thinking is distorted.

Distorted thinking causes you to be blind to reality and see yourself and the world in a negative way - you are constantly putting yourself down and not giving yourself credit for your accomplishments. Everything that goes wrong or doesn't work out is all your fault, rather than partially or in some cases mostly due to circumstances beyond your control. You blame yourself for everything because you no longer feel that you are good enough; the breakup pulled the rug out from under you and you're having a hard time standing firmly on the ground. You are your own worst critic and this irrational thinking pattern causes you to undermine yourself. You apply labels to yourself that are inaccurate and harsh. You have an unbalanced view of yourself, the world, and the people around you, including your ex.

One type of distorted thinking that is particularly harmful is making overgeneralizations. For example: Three of your relationships may have failed, so you stop dating because you assume that doing so would be a waste of time. You simply throw up your hands in frustration and give up because you think that your relationships are doomed to fail, which becomes a self-fulfilling prophecy. But the reality is totally different – when you sit down and think about everything rationally, you discover that the real reason those three relationships didn't work out was because one man moved to a different city, another was still involved with an ex-girlfriend, and the last man you dated had financial troubles, was depressed about his situation, and wasn't open to love, so he shut you out. Many things can happen to cause a relationship to end that aren't remotely close to being 100% your fault. But if you continue telling yourself that your luck is bad you'll never regain the confidence to make an effort to stay in the game and eventually meet the right person. If this is your thinking pattern stop it now. Avoid using sentences like, "Things never work out for me," or, "My relationships always fail." What you're telling yourself is untrue. Instead, replace this thinking pattern with, "I haven't met the right person yet, and I will continue to be open," or, "I know that all men are different people with different personalities and needs. I also know that circumstances beyond my control can positively or negatively affect a relationship." The opposite of this thinking pattern is when you feel like you are a victim and everything that happens to you is the fault of someone else. This mindset is even more detrimental because it keeps you from gaining self-insight, so you repeat behavior that is unhelpful.

Another harmful thinking pattern is when you view the world in extremes. Do you live in a black and white world with no shades of gray? When you categorize everything and everybody sharply in your mind the world becomes a hostile place. An example of this thinking pattern is when you tell yourself: "He was the only one for me and now he's gone forever," as if there were no other men in the world. Out of the billions of men on the planet and the millions living close to you, I'm sure that there is someone living nearby who would be a wonderful match for you, although they won't magically come to you, and you'll have to make an effort to find that person. But if you think in extremes it will hamper your efforts and hold you back. When you meet other men, you'll eventually find someone interesting who you will want to continue seeing. And you don't know for sure that your ex is gone forever. He might show up on your doorstep one day, something that would be unfortunate, but it could happen. People are complex, and no definitive assumptions should be made about what their actions will be in the future.

Do you apply labels to yourself and others? For example: You've put on ten pounds and your clothing no longer fits. Rather than eat less and walk more, you label yourself as fat. Because you are applying a negative label to yourself, you lose the confidence to get out of the house and date. What you should do is buy yourself a couple of new outfits that fit you well, actively try and meet men to date, and while dating you can join a gym and get back the body you had before the weight gain.

Negative thinking patterns, although limiting, brings a person relief from their situation in the short-term because fewer risks are taken while they are stagnating. But in the long-term this thinking is extremely damaging. It's easy to blame yourself for everything that goes wrong and not do a thorough analysis of what happened and why. It's also easy to stay attached to the dreamy, unrealistic memory of your ex and not go through the trouble of finding someone new. You will experience some discomfort when you let go of his memory and make a genuine effort to live your life without him. But once the discomfort fades, when you realize that you are the master of your life and not all those negative thoughts holding you back, you will have triumphed.

Breakup Survival
Summaries

- When we're in love we look for our love interest's good qualities and blind ourselves to the bad. Because we do this, after a breakup we are often confused.
- The writing exercise in this chapter will help you to reach an epiphany and you will achieve closure because you'll be able to answer your own questions.
- After doing the exercise, store your lists somewhere you can find them so that you can refer to them in the future if necessary.
- Rid yourself of negative thinking patterns that hold you back in life.

Chapter Ten

How to Get Through That One Horrible Day

The process of getting over a breakup is like driving down a road you've never driven before – because it's unfamiliar territory, you don't always see potholes and bumps, so sometimes driving turns rough. But if you accept that you will be hit with situational depression at times the road becomes smoother, and eventually you'll be able to drive on safely without incurring any serious damage. This way of thinking offers a great deal of protection, but even so, along the way, it's not unusual for someone to have one or more difficult days where they are completely stymied and unable to function at all. This day could occur during the first month after the breakup or even farther down the road such as a year later. Getting through this lousy day is much easier if you understand what you're going through, why it's happening, and how to pull through it. There are seven simple steps you can take listed below:

Step 1: Find a quiet place so that you can process what's happening. If you're at work, take your lunch break at a park or away from the crowd. If you're at school, you can go to the library and sit in a private study room if one is available.

Step 2: Once you're comfortably situated, breathe in through your nose gently and exhale slowly through your mouth. Do this four or five times. This breathing exercise will relax your mind and body immediately.

Step 3: Ask yourself what you're feeling and why. When you pinpoint the stressor, you will be less anxious. Defining the problem is the key to feeling better because confusion breeds more anxiety. If you have a pen and paper handy, you can write it down. Or, you can enter the information into the memo section of your cellphone.

Step 4: Accept that you're having a bad day and that you know why. Allow your mind to process this information. Everyone has good and bad days. Few people have a string of good days in a row. Most people have crappy days in between good ones, or a string of crappy days and then a string of better ones. That's just how life is and no one, no matter how attractive, successful, or smart can escape that fact.

Step 5: Ask yourself if the issue that is causing you stress will matter in a month, a year, or five years from now. Most likely, it won't. But if you think that it might affect you in the long-term, write down why you believe that to be the case and what you can do to turn it around. Take action if you think it's necessary, but do so in a smart way. Oftentimes, problems resolve themselves or become less urgent over time and no action is needed.

Step 6: Keep yourself from obsessing about the specific problem or problems that are affecting you during the day by absorbing yourself in your work or studies. When you return home, read over the list you made with all the ideas you had to keep yourself distracted. If there's nothing on it that pops out at you, add some more ideas that you think would work. You might also choose to call a friend so that you don't feel alone.

Step 7: Accept the fact that in life things are constantly changing. If you look back in time you'll realize that clothing styles have dramatically changed over the years, as well as music, and culture. Jobs that were once common no longer exist due to technological advances, and new jobs are being created all the time. Tomorrow brings change and things will be different – this is a certainty. Allow yourself to be flexible – similar to how a flower blows in the wind, and remain open-minded. Have confidence that you will get through this difficult time and that things will surely get better. That way you won't get so caught up in the moment.

Overcoming the Feeling of Being in a Dark Place

The personal story that I will share with you now might seem heavy, but I'm doing it to make an important point – that even when you're hit with one disappointment after another, you can turn things around for the better and enjoy life again.

During the worst breakup of my life with a man that I had been engaged to, I was also given some bad news about my health. Because of the length of time it took me to deal with my illness, I ended up having to leave my job. I was faced with the triple-whammy of losing my partner in life who I loved deeply, having poor health, and losing my livelihood. My occupation was what gave me an identity – a reason to feel proud and accomplished, so losing it and then finding out that I had been replaced was hard. My job had also kept me from thinking about my failed relationship, and since I no longer had a place to go every day, I obsessed about my ex. Going through treatment was difficult, and I had to do it alone. I experienced financial difficulties, could barely cover my bills, and was unable to purchase the home I had saved for years to buy. The world felt unfriendly and I began to feel like an outsider. I would watch people commuting to and from work from my window while I had to stay at home or go to doctor's appointments. On the days I felt slightly better and was able to leave the house, I would walk past restaurants and see couples enjoying a night out together inside – seeing this was a reminder that I had no one. I had the sense that life was something that other people were meant to enjoy, but not me. I felt trapped by the parameters I set for myself – I boxed myself in believing that my present situation would also be my future.

When I was home alone, I would sometimes recall an evening in my early-teens when my friend talked me into going to a nightclub – this memory, that originally had no meaning, ended up meaning everything to me. I had lost track of this friend, but occasionally my sister would mention her when talking about events from our childhood – this is likely what first triggered the memory.

The night my friend and I went to the nightclub we had no ID, and since we were underage, we should not have been allowed inside. Once we entered, I found the environment to be dark and sleazy. The music at that particular club was terrible, so rather than finding it entertaining as I had expected, to me it was deafening – I stuck tissue in my ears so that I could tolerate the noise. The drinks that different men ordered for me made me nauseous, and I sat with people I found scary or by myself for hours while my friend danced. I saw a glowing exit sign in the back, invitingly beckoning me to escape my situation. I sat and stared at it, as if it was the answer to my problem.

When going through my difficulties there were days when that exit sign would stick out in my mind, informing me that I had a way out. I wanted desperately to escape the devastation I felt due to the breakup, my sick body, and the emptiness and continuous struggle that was my life. I would think to myself: Make it stop. I want out. But then my mind would turn to something else that happened on that night, long ago. I realized my mistake in having gone to the club at such a young age. I approached my friend on the dance floor and told her that I was going to leave with or without her. And, to my surprise, she chose to leave with me – through the front door. We ended up going to a restaurant, met up with friends, and had a great time. I often use that analogy when I think about my life and how things ended up unfolding - the choice I made as a teenager was similar to what I did after being dumped by my fiancé and then becoming sick. I was in a nightmare situation and wanted out, but I chose to face the problem and found a solution. When getting over my breakup, because I set the ground rules for my own recovery, I was able to put the relationship behind me. Soon after, my health returned, and things fell into place once again. I had to be patient and work towards pulling myself up by my bootstraps, but I was able to do it. I still have bad days like everyone else, but the good far outweigh the bad. The man that left me came back, but I rejected his advances because although he knew that I was sick, he offered me no help or sympathy, and in my eyes, he bad character. I dated once I got my confidence back and met someone else.

No one is immune from having their partner leave them or getting an unexpected illness. What happened to me can happen to anyone. There are periods in people's lives where they have to fight to keep going, but fighting through difficulties teaches us lessons and widens our minds. During my darkest days I tried to keep myself distracted so that I wouldn't sink further into depression - I decided to create lists which I utilized, and they were effective. I got out of the house as much as I could and met people face-to-face so that I had regular human contact. I learned new skills and started a small business. I exercised when I was able, and it helped pull me out of depression. I did everything I had to do to help myself, and those nuisance gray clouds that seemed to always hang over my head slowly lifted, one cloud at a time. I wouldn't wish what happened to me on anyone else. But I can say from personal experience that you *can* remake your life.

Breakup Survival
Summaries

- Understanding that you will experience situational depression occasionally while getting over a breakup will help you deal with the bumps on the road on your way to healing.

- Most people will experience at least one extremely difficult day where the stress and anxiety due to the breakup make it hard for them to function. Combined with other difficulties a person might be going through at the same time, the stress a person feels can seem overwhelming.

- You can get through a tough day by following some simple steps that will relax you and help you gain your perspective back.

- Find a quiet place to sit and process what is happening to you. Perform a gentle, slow, breathing exercise to lower the stress you feel immediately.

- Define the problem that's bothering you because once you know exactly what is causing your anxiety, you can face it.

- Accept the fact that you'll have good days and bad days, just like everyone else.

- Ask yourself if the problem causing you stress is a short or long-term issue. If you think that it will affect you in the future, think of a way that you can turn it around. Decide to take intelligent action or allow the problem to resolve itself over time.

- To get through the day so that you can start fresh tomorrow, look over the list you made of ideas you can use to distract yourself. You might also choose to call a friend so that you don't feel alone.

- Change is constant and few things in life remain the same. Tomorrow will be different than today.

Chapter Eleven

The Detachment Phase

At some point you will begin to feel a level of detachment from your ex. Once this kicks in, it's important that you allow yourself to follow this state of mind. The beauty of detachment is that it frees you from painful memories. You'll remember what happened, but it will no longer take as big a toll on you emotionally. You'll still think about him, but not every day. And if you begin to obsess about him again you'll have the ability to snap yourself out of it. During this phase of recovery, it's easy to fall into a state of boredom; transitions are often dull. You are used to having intense feelings, but now there is no longer that sense of excitement and curiosity.

The worst thing to do when you're feeling blah is to try and shake things up. Some people are uncomfortable with the feeling of detachment and become disturbed by their lack of emotion; they feel the need to get their heart pounding again. They might contact their ex under the guise of making peace with him, or to suggest a friendship. This is a huge mistake and totally self-defeating. Anyone who does this is putting themselves right back where they started - the first stages of recovery.

The people who recover most quickly from a breakup are those who don't fight detachment. Grudge holders have terrible difficulty getting over a breakup because they take most things personally and don't allow themselves to feel detached. Luckily, most people have the ability to forgive others and themselves and can naturally reach this phase. It's also important when trying to get over a breakup to keep your ego in check because to reach the detachment stage it's necessary to leave your ego at the door. In everyday life a level of narcissism is good. To get ahead in this world you need to believe in yourself and your abilities. But when trying to get over a breakup, instead of helping you it will work against you. If your ego takes a massive hit whenever you experience rejection or fail to reach a goal, you will suffer a lot more than you have to.

The Awkward In-Between Stage

It's not unusual to have fantasies about making an ex jealous. You dream about bumping into him while you're on a date with a man who is taller or more handsome. You post photos of yourself on social media sitting next to a male friend while wearing a sexy dress, hoping to drive your ex crazy with jealousy. Attempting to show-up an ex can give you a momentary ego boost, but in the end, it's a meaningless exercise because the relationship is over anyway. When you begin to feel detached and no longer think about him every day like you did before, you will still have these fantasies at times, but they will go away eventually. Because detachment is a natural process, you might not even realize it's happening. Your life will go on and other interests will develop. One day, he will slip from your mind altogether and you'll be over him.

Here are a few signs that will tell you when you've gotten over your ex:

1. You no longer fantasize about bumping into him when you're out with a male friend or on a date.
2. You've deleted him from the contacts list in your cellphone and no longer see his profile photo pop up on the messaging apps you used to communicate with him.
3. You're not interested in checking his social media posts to see if he's in a new relationship and what he's been up to.
4. You've stopped hoping that you will someday get back together with him.
5. You no longer read his horoscope hoping to tap into what's going on in his life.
6. You're in a new relationship with someone you genuinely care about; you're not on the rebound.
7. When you see your ex out in public with a woman, it doesn't devastate you. You don't put much energy into wondering whether she's his colleague, a relative, or date.
8. He might live or work nearby, but you no longer feel his presence as you go about your day.

9. You're driving down the street and see a car whizzing by that looks like your ex's car. You're curious to know if it's him or not, but your curiosity isn't strong enough to make you react - your heart doesn't pound faster, and you don't seriously consider driving back to take a look. Instead, you drive on thinking about all the things you have to do that day.

Breakup Survival
Summaries

- At some point you will begin to feel detached from your ex. Go with this feeling and don't fight it.
- Being detached might feel boring, but it's a good thing.
- When you've gotten over the breakup, you will no longer wish to get back together with him or fantasize about making him jealous. If you bump into him when he's out with another woman it won't devastate you as it would have in the past.
- Eventually, you'll reach a point where you're completely detached, meaning you're over him.

Chapter Twelve

Why Breakups Have Become More Traumatic

Although breakups have always been difficult, the usage of messaging apps and social networks, as with most technological advances throughout history, have had unintended consequences. It's so easy for people to communicate quickly using their devices that many have become lazy and rarely make time for face-to-face human interaction, viewing it as an inconvenience that drags them away from work or out of the house. These two modes of communication leave people unable to detect subtle inflections in people's voices, or read their facial expressions and body language making it harder for them to understand one another's true feelings. Messaging apps have effectively taken much of the formality out of dating and promoted the usage of slang, further eroding romance. Video calls are wonderful and allow for better communication than traditional voice calls. However, the easy access of video-mode puts pressure on people to look their best at odd hours of the day when they might be tired or standing in bad lighting.

New techniques have been mastered for dumping people showing a lack of empathy that was rare before the global usage of apps and social networks made it easier for people to flit casually in and out of each other's lives. Being able to communicate with complete strangers on various networks, people have the false sense that they have and endless choice of partners, and many will play games with the people they're dating in order to keep their options permanently open. When these games are played from the outset, deep relationships rarely develop, and breakups are a guessing game. People are left wondering if their relationships were ever real, if they were really dumped, and if their exes will pop up one day unexpectedly and behave as if they were old pals. Cold terms are now commonly used to describe the ambiguity of the situation people find themselves in after being dumped and what is perpetuated by the "dumper." Some of these terms are: ghosting, zombie-ing, benching, haunting, putting someone on ice, cushioning, and placing someone on simmer. There is a good chance that during your dating life you've experienced one of the infamous techniques described in detail below. The first four are somewhat new while the last three are old-school classics that have been renamed

- **Ghosting, also known as "vanishing":** When someone wants to instigate a breakup, but can't face the other person they will simply disappear from their life without warning. The person doing the ghosting wants a double-win for themselves – they wish to exit without the sticky inconvenience of a confrontation, while at the same time they want the ability to come back to the person they dumped at a later time if they feel like it because technically, there was no definitive ending. The individual they unexpectedly ceased communicating with is supposed to take the hint that they've been dumped, but be appreciative of the fact that things are being left open.

- **Zombie-ing:** This is a term used to describe the actions of an ex who ghosted you, but pops up months or even years later by sending you a casual chat message, or leaving a comment on your social media page. Essentially, your ex, who you long buried and left in the past suddenly wakes from the dead and begins conversing with you as if you hung out recently and are the best of friends. When this happens it usually means that he has recently come out of a relationship and is looking for intimacy with a familiar woman, or he has been in several failed relationships and likely views each woman from his past as a "friend" that he can store in his contacts list for a future rendezvous if she's up for it. If one woman he reaches out to shoots him down, he's got others on file. Zombie-exes who come back in this manner tend to ghost women as a pattern, so it's risky to begin seeing a man who crawls out of his coffin to reconnect. Can a man who tends to ghost women and then rise like a zombie ever find real love? Yes, it's possible, but only if he gains self-insight and breaks his pattern.

- **Benching:** A commitment-phobic person who doesn't want to feel alone will often date someone they choose to rarely see face-to-face, conducting their relationship mostly on their smartphone. This type of person might be intimate with you a few times in a scattered way and give you all sorts of excuses why they can't see you regularly in person. Yet, at the same time, they shower you with friendly and flattering chat messages so that you don't walk away from them. This sort of behavior seriously messes with the mind of the person on the receiving end of it because at the beginning, they genuinely believe that the bencher is just super-busy. The person who is being benched wants a relationship with the bencher, but since it never really happens they are often strung along for months or years, hoping for something that never truly materializes. If, in the future, you see that your relationship is taking place mostly online, know that you are being benched or otherwise being held at arm's length for a reason that only the bencher knows.

- **Haunting:** This occurs after a breakup when the person who was dumped begins noticing comments on their social media page from their ex. The haunter is attempting to reconnect casually but not trying to get back together because if he wanted to do that he would call or send a chat message, both higher levels of communication. He might be seeking attention, hoping for a response that will stroke his ego. Or, he feels guilty about the breakup and wants his ex to respond in a mild or friendly way so that he doesn't feel so bad about how he treated her. The kindest thing to do would be to leave the woman he dumped alone, but he lacks empathy and is too selfish to realize this.

- **Putting someone on ice:** This is the act of starting a relationship with someone, and then backing away so that a real commitment is never made. But no breakup is instigated, and contact is still made occasionally, usually after weeks or months have gone by, giving the person on the receiving end the sensation that they are being stored for later use. People who put others on ice are attempting to keep their options open while dating, or they might not know exactly what they are looking for in a partner. They become romantically involved with a woman because they don't want to be alone, or they are dating more than one person and putting them all in the freezer when it suits them. They find the woman they are placing on ice attractive or they wouldn't have started dating her in the first place, but they aren't absolutely certain that she is the one for them. They believe that when they find the right person they will know it, but this turns out not to be the case in the long-run and they often regret putting a woman on ice who they later realize was "the one that got away."

- **Cushioning:** This phenomenon occurs when someone who is in a relationship that is unsatisfying begins to date before they are emotionally or financially ready to leave their partner. They date so that they will have other people on standby should they grow the balls to exit their situation. But feeling comfortable, and concerned about the fallout if they actually left, they end up wasting the time of the women they date who believe that they are single or in the process of ending a difficult relationship. The women get the sense that they've been put on ice but rarely realize that they are being used as cushions.

- **Placing someone on simmer:** This is an attempt at a slow breakup. The special person in your life communicates with you less and less over time, similar to a downward sliding scale, hoping that you will become frustrated and exit the situation so that they don't have to feel guilty about dumping you. They start the process by calling and making plans with you less and less over several weeks or months, like air slowly being let out of a balloon. Eventually, you notice that all the recent plans you made as a couple were cancelled and realize that you are supposed to simply accept the fact that you've been dumped.

Eventually, people who play games and break up with others in the ways discussed above end up experiencing the same thing themselves and are hurt too - this is the world they live in. This vicious cycle of insensitivity erodes trust and also makes it harder to rekindle relationships because people become afraid to let their guard down from the get-go.

When someone rejects another person romantically, they are showing them kindness and respect by letting them down once, and being direct about it. Popping in and out of someone's life is a cruel tease and should never be done – it displays the worst sort of insensitivity. People often say that in love there are no rules, but there are – these are the rules you set for yourself. It might appear to you that everyone is behaving in a similar way and that you have to put up with it because unless you do, you will be alone. But guess what – when you're with someone who plays mind-games, you are alone anyway. It's like having an imaginary friend instead of a lover. In the future, if you begin to feel that a man you're involved with is playing games with you, or you sense that he's ambivalent, you can simply ask him, "Would you like to remain in this relationship with me, or do you want out?" By saying this you're letting him know that you are aware of his ambivalence and want him to make a decision so that he doesn't drag you along an empty highway for months or years. This allows you to clear the path for someone who is sure about you and who you can develop a tangible connection with. To protect yourself from all the soul-draining nonsense, communicate with the next man you become involved with mainly in person and limit the time you spend chatting with him using your phone.

Breakup Survival Summaries

- One of the unintended consequences of smartphone usage is that these devices have made the quality of human interaction much poorer than it was before. Hiding behind messaging apps and conversing on platforms, people have become desensitized to one another's feelings and needs. For this same reason, breakups have become crueler and uglier.
- People fade in and out of each other's lives creating an ambiguous environment that leaves people wondering if their relationships are stable.
- People now break up with each other in ways that they would have been chastised for in the recent past. But they get away with it because it appears that everyone else is doing the same thing. There is no reasonable excuse for showing a lack of sensitivity towards others, but unfortunately, this behavior is now more accepted than it was in the past by society.
- Communicate less on your phone and more in person with the next man you become involved with so that you can develop something real and meaningful.

Chapter Thirteen

The Complexities of Getting Back Together with an Ex and Why It Rarely Works Out

After a breakup, no matter how hard you try to erase your ex from your memory, he will remain in the forefront of your mind for several weeks or months. But as time goes by, he will slip slowly backward, little by little, until his memory reaches the back corners of your mind, although some trace of him will likely always remain. As you go about your life, memories will be triggered by events happening or by your surroundings. You might decide to paint your bedroom a new color, and even though you think that a certain shade of blue would look best, you will avoid using it because it was your ex's favorite color. Or, your friends will suggest taking a trip to Las Vegas, but you will tell them that you are unable to join them, not because you're busy, but because you were married in that city and just being there might depress you. This sort of visceral reaction could happen even twenty years after your divorce. However, memories that pop up every few years don't mean that you want to get back together with your ex, or that you have feelings of love or hatred towards him that you've carried for a long time. It simply means that he occupies some tiny territory in your head. Most people, as they grow older, become accustomed to this and accept it as a part of life. But not everyone is the same, and although rare, sometimes a person will reach out to an ex because they want to rekindle an old flame or simply want to be friends. But whatever their desired outcome, rarely do things turn out as they imagined

What makes a person consider getting back together with their ex?

- After a failed relationship, a person might reflect on what occurred that caused their breakup and view their ex in a more positive light. They might come to the conclusion that what they walked away from was worth fighting for. If they choose to contact their ex and that individual still has feelings for them too, they might be able to get back together.
- After having been in other relationships, a person might reminisce about a past relationship. If the memory of a first love or a romantic interest from years ago still haunts them, they might reach out to that person. If their past love is available and interested, it's possible that something can develop.
- When someone is in an unfulfilling relationship, they might come to the realization that an

earlier relationship was far better, and regret having given up on it. They might contact their ex and request a second chance. This situation can be terribly messy, and a lot of upheaval can occur because one or both people involved might be married.

- Sometimes a memory is triggered in someone's mind that they can't shake. They get a surge of feeling and want to meet up with their ex to relive memories that over the years became important to them.

- Many people are walking around still thinking about "The one that got away." They continue to dream about an ex who they felt was a quality person and had desirable attributes. They regret not having appreciated this person's wonderful qualities when they were in the relationship and might decide to contact them, hoping for another chance.

- Someone who directed most of their energy towards their career or educational goals might regret not taking a past relationship seriously; they may have had a casual relationship with someone they cared for but chose not to take it a step further. Once they've reached their goals and their mind becomes clearer, they begin to think about that person and reach out to them.

Why are most couples unable to reconcile?

- If one person wishes to reconcile with a past love, but their love interest is in a happy relationship, reconciliation is unlikely to occur.

Both people must want to get back together at the same time.

- When someone tries to get their ex back using aggressive tactics, their ex might switch off emotionally, shutting them out completely. Making public scenes, being overly dramatic, stalking, contacting them several times a week, or messaging them non-stop will make it less likely that the relationship will ever be rekindled because the person on the receiving end will want to escape the stress of it all.

- After a breakup, if one person contacts the other on a regular basis under the guise of friendship, it gives their ex no room to realize their loss.

- Some people take the attitude of: What's done is done. They look forward, never backward, and cannot be convinced to try again.

- If one person behaves in a hot and cold manner during a relationship, meaning that they get together with their partner in fits and starts, it can create a situation where their partner literally doesn't know if they are even *in* a relationship. The uncertainty of their situation eventually causes them to look elsewhere for attention and affection. By the time the person who is hot and cold realizes that their relationship has fizzled, their love interest is with someone new and cannot be convinced to return to an unstable situation.

- When attraction is strong, and a great deal of passion exists between two people, but they are not connected in any other way, if their relationship ends it is unlikely that it can be revived. Physical attraction is fantastic, but it doesn't equal something lasting, and it can't be the only basis for a relationship. There also needs to be trust, respect, and the two people should have mutual interests.

- Lifestyle issues and personal preferences about where to live and whether to have children are important for every couple to discuss. Sometimes, two people are in love but desire totally different things in life. This means that if they break up, getting back together will not be plausible.

- If one person cheated and that's why the relationship ended - because of a lack of trust - it can be incredibly difficult to build that trust again.

- One bad memory can remain in a person's head for a lifetime. Although people tend to remember the good times and try to forget the bad, if an ex contacts them out of the blue they might weigh the good against the bad. If their ex comes up short on what they view as the good side, they will avoid that person.

- If there was verbal abuse, or worse, one person became violent at some point during the relationship the chance that it can be rekindled are slim, understandably. No one should ever consider getting back together with someone who was abusive towards them.

Couples that get back together, separate, and then get back together again are doing what I call "ping-ponging." This pattern can occur for several reasons: There might be a highly charged chemistry between two people, and although they don't get along outside of the bedroom and are aware on some level that they're wasting each other's time, they don't have the strength to walk away completely. It might be that neither person can find a new partner after their breakup who meets their needs, so they get back together with their ex, but then realize for the umpteenth time that it was a mistake. When two people engage in ping-ponging, the drama it creates can throw their lives off course, and even damage their health and ability to earn a living. If a couple tries once and fails, trying another time is not a far-fetched idea if both are willing to make concessions. But getting back together several times often wastes precious time and leads to sheer misery for the couple themselves and everyone around them, including their friends and family who will eventually say to them while rolling their eyes, "Oh, no. Not him again!"

Breakup Survival Summaries

- Sometimes a person will reminisce about a past relationship and contact their ex. When they do, usually the timing is off by months or years and the relationship can't be revived due to a variety of reasons.
- Relationships can rarely be rekindled because both people must want to get back together at the exact same time for this to occur. Usually, after some time has passed, at least one person will have begun a relationship with someone new, or they will decide that they don't want to try a second time with their ex.
- It's not unheard of for couples to get back together, but both people must be willing to make concessions for it to work. Not everyone has the diplomatic skills to pull this off.
- Getting back together with an ex and then breaking up again several times eventually becomes a foolish endeavor.

Chapter Fourteen

Your Ex Resurfaces

The Guessing Game

Most men, when they want to reconnect with an ex-girlfriend will approach her in a non-aggressive way. If the woman hasn't changed her phone number, a man might use a messaging app to send her a simple chat message such as, "Hi, how are you?" If he doesn't get the response he wants or is ignored, a phone call is usually the next step. When an ex contacts you, the conversation is unlikely to go smoothly and will be choppy at best.

If your ex were to contact you, it might play out like this: You're on your way home from work and your cellphone rings – you answer, and realize it's him. You noticed that he left a friendly comment on your social media page three days earlier, but you didn't know how to respond to it because you weren't sure what it meant, so you did nothing. There is a long pause over the phone as you wait for him to speak. When he finally does, he asks you what you've been up to lately. You tell him basic details about what's been going on in your life, but he doesn't seem to be listening. He then tells you that he's been thinking about you and doesn't like the way things ended. You tell him that you feel the same way. But just when you think he might ask you to get back together, he changes the subject. You get the impression that he wants to know if you're seeing someone else, but he doesn't ask you outright. Your polite conversation continues awkwardly until there is another long pause. As quickly and unexpectedly as he called, he tells you that he has to go; he then says goodbye and hangs up. After this brief interaction, you are either left feeling elated because he's just admitted that he's still thinking about you, or upset and angry that he called. Calls like this from an ex are not uncommon. He's hoping to reconnect, but his motives are murky. Maybe he'll call again and attempt to reconcile. Or, he might choose to call the one time and never call again. Both are strong possibilities and it's hard to guess what he might do next. He might not even have a clear idea of why he called; he may have simply felt compelled. It's not unusual for people to feel confused about their emotions after a breakup. Some of what you went through he's likely to have experienced too. Breakups are rarely clean events where both people write each other off and move on. There are moments when people miss their ex, and moments when they're glad that the relationship ended.

It's a good idea to have a plan in case he calls. If he were to phone you at a time when you were able to speak freely, you could take the initiative and tell him about any regrets you have, and allow him to do the same. Doing so might not have its intended effect; he might not respond the way you'd like him to. However, expressing yourself is helpful when trying to achieve closure if you're lucky enough to have the opportunity. If he suggests getting back together you should ask him why in a diplomatic way. Also, ask him what would be different this time.

Know What's in Your Best Interest

Because you won't know the reason for his call unless he tells you, it would be best to accept that he called and do nothing. If he has something he needs to say, he'll contact you again. If the two of you have been apart for at least a few weeks you should be able to put on your rational thinking cap. You will probably have an immediate, visceral response to a call from him. If it's irritation or anger you won't need to do any soul-searching. You can be confident in the fact that you don't want to have contact with him again. If you have a sentimental response, or your heart races with hope that you might get back together, take some time to check your emotions. The best way to do this is to refer to your four lists (the exercise from **Chapter Nine**). Read them over carefully and let the words sink in. After reading your lists, set them aside and do some thinking.

How do you feel about him now? Do you know in your heart that if you were to give him a second chance, you would only end up right back where you are now – getting over another breakup with him? If you broke up because he cheated on you, can you get past it? And, do you trust him not to do it again? If he broke up with you by vanishing unexpectedly, isn't it likely that he would repeat that behavior?

Four Things to Consider:

1. You've already been in a relationship with this person and it ended. If you were to estimate a chance of the relationship succeeding a second time around, what percentage would you assign to that? Is it 50%? Or, is it as low as 20%? Assign a percentage that sounds right to you. By making this judgment you're not being an optimist or pessimist. You're being a realist. If you think that there would be a slim chance that the relationship would survive, why try again?

2. A man will sometimes contact an ex-girlfriend because he has no one in his life at a particular time that he can be intimate with or he feels nostalgic. Choosing to contact a woman he already knows is much easier than seeking out a new partner. But starting an intimate relationship with an ex rarely leads to a full reconciliation. In fact, I've coined a phrase for this situation – I call it the "incomplete return."

3. When you're in a relationship, you are off the market. If you see no long-term, tangible future with your ex, why start seeing him again and close the door on dating other men?

4. Your time is precious. Don't waste it with someone who isn't the right person for you. If you are always arguing, worrying, and feeling stressed and upset, it's not a satisfying relationship. Why spend your life suffering? You can find someone else and have

113

a chance at a secure relationship that adds quality to your life instead of draining your energy and making you miserable.

If your ex is calling you and you're flirting with the idea of seeing him again, remember that you broke up for a reason. Consider everything that happened in the past and make the assumption that if you were to take him back you would be living with similar, if not the exact same conditions. You are free to do what's in your best interest. There's no rule book that says you owe this man anything.

Breakup Survival Summaries

- Being contacted by an ex out of the blue is not uncommon. Sometimes it means something, and other times it holds no real significance.
- If his call makes you irritated or angry, you'll know that no matter how he feels it's definitely over for you. If his call makes your heart race, take the time to do a reality check.
- Pull out your four lists from **Chapter Nine** and read them over carefully.
- If you're considering seeing him again, know that if you were to do so, you would most likely be living with the same conditions as before the breakup.
- You have countless other options in life including the chance to date other men. Getting back together with your ex will get in the way of those opportunities.

Chapter Fifteen

Four Breakup Stories

Nina, Jessica, Katrina, and Carmen are four women who experienced traumatic breakups. Nina's boyfriend told her some unexpected news. Jessica's boyfriend suddenly became secretive. Katrina's boyfriend, who she knew from the past, started behaving strangely. And Carmen's relationship had been unwinding for months before she realized what was happening. All four women deal with the end of their relationships in very different ways.

Nina's Breakup

Michael, a thirty-three-year-old engineer, had recently proposed to Nina, a thirty-year-old hair stylist. Nina happily sported her engagement ring at work, and her clients smiled and gave her their warmest congratulations. Nina was feeling elated - she loved Michael deeply and was looking forward to spending her life with him. At the same time, her career was taking off and she was attracting more regular clients.

What Nina didn't share with her colleagues and clients was that Michael hadn't called her in nearly two weeks, which was highly unusual. In their two-year relationship the longest Michael had gone without contacting her was a week, and that was because he had been out of town. Nina's intuition told her that something wasn't right, so she tried to comfort herself by glancing at the glittering diamond on her ring-finger. Over the last few days she had sent Michael several chat messages from her cellphone, but he never replied. Frustrated and wondering why he was avoiding her, she sent an email to his work email address asking for his opinion about a wedding venue. She wanted their wedding, which was to be in eight months, to take place in Malibu. When Michael didn't respond to that either, Nina decided to call his office, but according to the receptionist he wasn't there. However, she said that he would be coming into work the next day and suggested she try his cellphone again. Nina left another chat message for Michael, asking him to contact her immediately. If he didn't, she wrote that she would stop by his office the next day to see if everything was okay.

Early that evening, Michael called Nina as she was walking home from work. He talked in circles for several minutes explaining how busy he had been lately. Then finally, he got to the point: Because of some work-related issues he would be too busy to plan a wedding. The timing was all wrong, he said.

Nina was stunned; unable to continue walking, she stood frozen in the middle of the sidewalk. "What? I don't understand. The wedding will be in eight months. Let's meet up and talk about this," she said.

"Nina, I won't be able to tonight. I'm having dinner with a colleague. He's flown a long distance to meet me and I can't get out of it."

"What happened?" she asked, choking on her words. She moved to the edge of the sidewalk so that other people could pass and leaned up against the wall of an office building. At that moment, she felt that if she didn't have the wall to lean on, she might have fallen over.

"I'm committed to some projects. I'm under a lot of pressure. And I'm just not ready for this. I'm sorry, but I think it's best that we stop seeing each other."

Nina felt like pinching herself to see if she was dreaming – if that was the case, she would wake up from her nightmare. But unfortunately, it wasn't a dream. "This can't be happening!" she said, her voice wavering. Then Nina, normally confident and composed, slid down the wall. "Michael? Are you still there?" she asked, but he'd ended the call. Moments later, she realized that she was sitting in a puddle of dirty water.

The day after Michael broke up with Nina, she cancelled a morning appointment and drove over to his office. The traffic was the worst she had ever seen, and she reached her destination an hour later than her planned time. After parking her car, she entered the building where Michael worked and hopped onto an elevator that took her to the second floor. When she reached the front door of his office she left him a chat message on his cellphone, informing him that she was there and about to enter. When he didn't respond within five minutes, she called him. He answered and asked her to walk inside and take a seat. He promised that he would come out and speak with her.

Nina took a seat next to the reception desk and waited patiently for Michael. Anxiously crossing and then uncrossing her legs, she tried her best to remain calm. She had never come to his office uninvited before and knew that it was an aggressive move, but she wasn't going to back down until she knew exactly what was going on. When her anxiety reached a point where she could barely tolerate it, Michael finally entered the room. He asked her to join him at a café in the lobby so that they could talk. The serious look on his face made her realize he was genuinely concerned that she might make a scene and embarrass him.

Michael opened the door which led to the hallway, and Nina followed him to the elevators, walking behind him rather than next to him. He pressed the down-button and waited for the elevator without looking at her, as if they were strangers. When it arrived, it quickly filled with people. Michael, the tallest man on the elevator, looked handsome to Nina in his gray suit and silver textured tie. She studied his profile; his platinum-blonde hair glowed under the light and made him look younger than he was, although it was beginning to recede around the temples. His blue eyes that usually shined looked translucent and cold that day. As Michael kept his gaze on the elevator doors, never turning his head to look at her, Nina thought to herself, that this man, who stood just inches from her, was supposed to be her future husband – but not anymore. When the doors opened, people began getting off one by one. Nina and Michael exited in silence and didn't speak to each other until they entered the café and took a seat across from each other at an empty table. "I want to know what happened," Nina said.

Michael looked around, and then gestured with his hands in a downward motion, indicating that he would appreciate it if she kept her voice down. Leaning towards her over the table, in a hushed tone, he finally spoke. "This is what's going on. I've been offered a new position. It's overseas and will begin next week. I'll be working ten to fifteen-hour days nearly every day for the next six months, if not longer. It's a big opportunity. I knew that you wouldn't be able to come with me because of your work, or travel to many of the locations where I'll be working, even if you wanted to. If I had factored us into it, I would have had to turn it down. That led me to decide against marrying, or even being in a relationship now."

Nina shot back, her heart pounding, "And where would you be going that it would be impossible to be with me?"

As Michael attempted to form an answer in his mind, the waiter interrupted. They hadn't touched the menus in front of them, so they ordered coffee and asked him to return in a few minutes. Michael sat back in his chair and folded his arms across his chest. This gesture, as Nina understood, meant that he was closing himself off to her. Noticing an angry expression cross her face when he did this, he unfolded them. After a long pause, he explained that as a consultant he would first be traveling to Singapore, and after that, he would be traveling throughout Asia. At times, he would be far from a major city.

Nina listened intently, trying to digest everything Michael said. She recalled one of her clients, a well-known singer, who had recently asked her to go on tour with her. She would have traveled to several cities throughout Europe that she had always wanted to visit. Nina had been thrilled at the offer, but after some soul-searching, she'd turned it down. Nina was planning to open her own salon and was concerned that if she was gone for too long she would lose some of her regular clients. But more importantly, she would have missed Michael, and it would have negatively affected their relationship. He had been the main reason she chose not to accept the offer.

Michael began speaking again, pulling Nina back into the tension of the moment. "Nina, would you really leave your job? I'd never ask you to do something like that. It wouldn't be fair. If the first few assignments go well, I'll be staying overseas longer, possibly for a couple of years. I think we're both at a point in our careers where we're going in different directions."

Nina knew that she had lost control of the conversation. Michael obviously wanted to unload her and there was nothing she could do to keep him in her life. She felt like there was a brick wall separating them that couldn't be knocked down. She wondered if he was involved with someone else and was telling her this story in an attempt to cover it up. She made a mental note to find out the exact date he was leaving. She planned to call his office and make certain he'd told her the truth. She had always trusted him, but that trust was gone now. She imagined running into him at a grocery store they frequented as a couple, catching him with his new girlfriend as they walked down an aisle with their cart, and shouting, "Overseas job, my ass!" and pelting him with cereal boxes.

After being served their coffee, they sat awkwardly and silently. Nina wondered why she wasn't crying but figured she had cried enough the night before and her body needed time to make more tears. Now, Michael was the one who looked like he was going to cry; she could see his eyes tearing up as if he had finally realized that if he walked away it would be a loss for him too. Noticing this, Nina wanted to comfort him. She wanted to reach across the table and hold his hand. But then, she thought how ridiculous it would be to comfort the person who had devastated her. What was she going to tell her friends and her family? She felt humiliated and helpless, as if she had been tossed aside by Michael like a sack of garbage. He was walking away as if all the time they'd spent together meant nothing.

Nina, unconvinced by his argument, finally spoke. "You wanted to marry me one minute and the next you throw me away without a second thought? How am I supposed to react? I'm sure you'll be working with men who are married. Engineers are not all bachelors. It's ridiculous to say that you have to remain single because of a job."

Michael, wanting to make his point clear, spoke firmly. "Yes, I'm sure that some of the men I'll be working with will be married. But most will be locals and they won't be leaving their spouses behind for months at a time. I'm not looking at things the same way you are, and this was not a rash decision I made overnight. I've thought long and hard about it. I'm taking the job because I feel that it's a once in a lifetime opportunity. Do you really want to be stuck in a long-distance relationship with someone you never see? There's no way around this, Nina."

At that moment, one of Michael's colleagues approached the table and informed him that they were starting a meeting upstairs. Michael nodded, and then said to him, "Give me a few minutes."

Watching his colleague enter the elevator and realizing that he would have to rush the last few moments he had to spend with Nina, Michael began to feel the brunt of his decision in the pit of his stomach. He wished that he could both accept the job and be with her, but convinced himself that he had to make a choice and stick with it. "I have to go up now," he said, softly. He pulled his wallet out of his back pocket and left money on the table to pay for their coffee.

Fighting back tears and putting her hands over her face, Nina exclaimed, "I love you Michael. I'm devastated. I haven't done anything wrong. I don't deserve this!"

Michael, pained by her words, couldn't bear the situation any longer. It was possible that if he comforted her, he would be taken in by his feelings, so he tried to remain calm and distant. As he rose from his chair, he took in a deep breath. Exhaling in frustration he said, "I'm sorry Nina…I'm so sorry." He then turned around slowly and walked towards the elevators. Nina said nothing as he walked away.

Nina's experience with Michael devastated her, but to her surprise, it didn't leave her unable to function. For months, she kept herself distracted by immersing herself in her work. Making her clients happy was the only thing that mattered in her life. And being around people every day kept her from feeling lonely.

One year after the breakup, Nina took out a business loan and opened her own salon. After surviving the first year, she realized that it had a good chance of being successful and put all her efforts into making it better. Once she felt that her business was gaining momentum, she began to think about what she wanted out of life in the long-term and decided to start dating again. Nina dated several men over the next four years hoping for an emotional connection, but ended up not becoming seriously involved with any of them. Sometimes she wondered if she was afraid to become attached, and that's why she was purposefully looking for faults in each person. She realized that she had never allowed herself to grieve properly after the breakup with Michael, having thrown her heart and soul into her work immediately. Nina recalled several chat messages that Michael had sent her during the first three months after he'd left, and how sweet they were. In them, he had apologized and told her how much he missed her. Nina responded to all of them, hoping that she could convince him to come back to her. In her last message to Michael, she wrote: *I love you and miss you too. Please call me.* She waited to hear back from him, but he never responded.

Two more years passed before Nina finally met someone who made her feel the spark she needed to make a commitment. On a busy Tuesday afternoon at her salon, a blonde woman walked in, nearly in hysterics over a botched color-job. She approached the receptionist and asked if someone could give her advice about how to fix the problem. Nina had just finished with a client, so she approached the woman and began speaking with her. Lifting the side of her hair, she saw the brassiness and uneven patches immediately and understood why she was upset. The sympathetic tone in Nina's voice calmed the woman, so she decided to make an appointment. As Nina stood next to her at the reception desk, she turned to her right and noticed that there was a man standing behind her, leaning against the wall, next to the door. When she established eye contact with him, he approached her and introduced himself as Joe. He then pointed to the woman making the appointment and said that her name was Arielle.

Nina thought that Joe and Arielle made an attractive couple – they appeared to be in their mid-thirties and were relaxed in each other's company. Smiling warmly, Nina invited them to take a seat on a black leather sofa to discuss the correction procedure and the costs. Nina pulled up a chair across from them and began speaking with Arielle, but oddly, all the while she was talking, she could see Joe sitting directly across from her staring, glued to her. It seemed as if he was flirting, in her opinion. She found him attractive and was flattered by his attention, but felt awkward because she assumed that Arielle was his wife.

After their conversation ended, Arielle looked at the time on her cellphone and rose to her feet. She told Nina how grateful she was that something could be done. And then she said, "Maybe Joe will drop by when I get my color fixed. He seems to be taken with you."

Confused by the comment, Nina looked over at Joe, whose cheeks were flushed. "He's welcome to drop by anytime," said Nina. Joe nodded politely at Nina and then opened the door for Arielle. The two smiled and waved goodbye as they exited.

During her appointment a week later, Arielle sat in Nina's chair and explained that she and Joe weren't married and had never dated. Nina, who was combing through and checking her hair carefully to make sure that the color had taken properly, listened as the outgoing Arielle chattered on nonstop. Arielle said that she was married to Martin, Joe's best friend, and that he and Joe produced documentary films together. Martin was in Brazil for three weeks and her car was in the shop, so to help her out while he was away, Joe had been kind enough to take her on errands. According to Arielle, Joe mentioned that he'd seen Nina out with some of her friends several weeks earlier at a restaurant, two blocks from her salon. He'd walked in for happy hour and noticed her sitting at a table - her red hair had stood out in the crowd. Joe claimed that he had been too shy to approach Nina because she was surrounded by a large group of people, but he took note of the fact that she wasn't wearing a ring. He was surprised when he saw her at the salon and thought that maybe she wore no ring because of her job. Arielle then asked Nina about her marital status. When she said that she was single, Arielle asked if she could give Joe her cellphone number, to which Nina replied, "Sure. That would be fine."

Joe called Nina the next day and asked her out for that upcoming Saturday. Nina, happy that he'd contacted her so soon, told him that she was free and asked him where he wanted to go on their date. Joe suggested they go to a film festival – he said that he wanted her to see his work in an environment where there was an engaged audience, something that he claimed was now a rarity. He wanted to begin their date in the afternoon so that they could enjoy the festival. Afterwards, he said that they could sit together privately at a restaurant and get to know each other.

Nina excitedly got dressed that Saturday afternoon and waited for Joe to pick her up at 3 o'clock. She chose a casual but form-fitting outfit which Joe admired as he walked with her from her front door to his car. At the festival they watched two films he had produced. Nina found both films interesting and insightful. Afterwards at dinner, she enjoyed their conversation. He was polite and chivalrous, unlike the men she had dated recently. Having enjoyed their date, when Joe dropped her off later that evening and asked her out again, she said yes to a second date.

On their next date, Nina showed Joe around her neighborhood and took him to her favorite café. To Nina's surprise, Joe ordered the exact same blend of coffee as she did. He even liked his the same way - with one teaspoon of sugar and no cream.

Joe and Nina enjoyed each others company so much that they fell into a dating pattern. After a year of dating steadily, Joe asked Nina to marry him, and she said yes. Joe rented out his home and moved into Nina's spacious apartment so that she could be close to her salon.

Joe continues to travel and produce films, and Nina has lessened her client load so that she can join him whenever one of his trips piques her interest. Two years into their marriage, Nina became pregnant with twins. Nina and Joe now have two beautiful daughters, Alexandra and Melissa.

Jessica's Breakup

Jessica, a twenty-eight-year-old buyer for a popular clothing company in the UK, had been dating Eric, a twenty-six-year-old real estate agent, for four years. They had been living together for a year and their lives blended effortlessly together, in Jessica's opinion. Feeling satisfied and secure in her relationship, Jessica had thought about testing the waters by asking Eric how he felt about settling down, but decided against pressuring him. She was sure that one day soon he would tell her that he wanted their situation to become permanent.

Home late after a long stressful day, Jessica stood in the kitchen preparing dinner for herself and asked Eric, who had gotten home before her that evening, if he'd eaten yet. Eric was sitting on the sofa fidgeting with his cellphone and didn't answer her, so she asked him the question again. Eric responded by telling her that he had already eaten and that she shouldn't worry about him. And then, he mumbled something unintelligible. When she asked him to repeat what he'd said, he exclaimed, "I'm moving out."

Jessica swung around, not sure if she had heard him correctly. "What? Are you joking? What did you say?" she asked. She immediately dropped what she was doing, walked over to the sofa, and sat down next to him. Eric was looking down at his phone and it took several seconds for Jessica to finally achieve eye contact with him. "What's this about?" she said.

Eric sighed and rolled his eyes in a way that Jessica would later come to view as arrogant and insensitive. He explained that he had felt constricted in their relationship for a long time, but he didn't know how to tell her this, so he had put it off many times. While listening to him, she briefly recalled a conversation they'd had when they first began dating about his wanting to be in a relationship, but also wanting to have his own space and not feel "trapped." She assumed long ago that the issue had been resolved. She didn't feel that she had been needy for attention or too clingy - she rarely called him at work, and she allowed him the freedom to go out with his friends whenever he wanted without argument. She wondered exactly what it was that was making him feel so "constricted."

Jessica sat silently and listened intently as Eric continued to rattle off his complaints. As he spoke, he became animated in his gestures, as if trying to convince himself rather than her that there were major problems in their relationship. He told her that he had been involved with her for four years, which he felt was a long time. And, although he claimed to love her, he explained that since he hadn't dated enough women, and she had been his only serious relationship, he couldn't be certain that she was the right person for him. After his rant, he looked at her blankly and admitted that he was confused.

Jessica and Eric sat for hours discussing their relationship, and the direction each believed it was going. Their discussion was civil until Eric said some hurtful things that she felt were unfair criticisms, and their conversation escalated into a shouting match. Finally, Eric explained that he had wanted to exit for a while, but had been fearful of a difficult confrontation. He complained that now he was getting the reaction that he had feared most. After telling her how sorry he was, he rose to his feet. "I can stay with Tom. He said he doesn't mind."

Jessica's head was pounding; she was too drained emotionally to speak with Eric any longer. Apparently, Tom knew more than she did about Eric's feelings and plans. Angry and frustrated, she told him that if he wanted to stay with Tom that he should go ahead. She rose from the sofa, entered the bathroom, and locked the door. Placing her hands on the sink counter, she began to cry, sobbing quietly so that Eric wouldn't hear her. Once she felt that she had cried enough, she looked at herself in the mirror and noticed that her eyeliner had migrated down her face, giving her a raccoon-like appearance.

"I'm going to pack some things now. I hope you're okay," Eric said, standing outside the door.

Jessica swallowed hard before answering him. "I'm fine. Why wouldn't I be?"

Outside, Jessica could hear Eric rushing around collecting his things and quickly shoving clothing into a duffle bag. He shouted something inaudible and then she heard the front door close. Jessica splashed water on her face and stared into the mirror again - water was dripping down her shirt, but she didn't care. Turning slowly, she opened the door. She then dragged herself out of the bathroom and into the bedroom. Looking around the room, her eyes fell on the closet door that had been left open; Eric had left most of his clothes behind. He had grabbed mostly casual clothing, but he'd also taken his favorite suit. Jessica opened the closet door wider. The smell of Eric's cologne lingered on his shirts, causing her to miss him immediately. She desperately wanted to go looking for him and bring him home, but she held herself back. Many of the things that he'd complained about were bogus, in her opinion. It was as if he was looking for whatever lame excuse he could find to leave her. She sat down on the edge of the bed and wracked her brain trying to figure out the real reason why he had walked out on her.

Eric's friend Tom had been contacting him a lot lately, and more than once he had put a female friend on the phone to speak with Eric. Oftentimes, these were video calls where Tom had his arm around a pretty young woman who looked like she'd had too much to drink and slurred her words. Tom was a regular at local hotspots and hotel bars around London. When he'd invited Eric to join him, Eric had usually brought Jessica along with him, and everyone had a nice time. However, Jessica recalled the last time they went out in a group, exactly one week ago - Tom's behavior was odd, and he'd pulled Eric aside several times in what appeared to be hushed, private conversations. She'd never asked Eric what the secretive talk had been about because it never occurred to her that it could have been anything serious. The name of one of the women that hovered around their table came to her mind - Fiona. She remembered Eric being overly friendly with her and began to wonder if Eric was already seeing her or some other woman and that was the real reason why he'd left. Lying back on the bed she'd shared with Eric, she stared up at the ceiling, tears streaming down the sides of her face. "Four years," she repeated to herself, as she cried.

The morning after Eric left, Jessica's face was puffy from crying. Unable to pull herself together enough to go to work, she called in sick claiming to have a cold. The woman who answered the phone at her office believed her excuse, told her that she sounded congested, and suggested she have some chicken soup. Wearing an old pair of baggy sweatpants, a torn t-shirt, and her hair in a lopsided ponytail, Jessica decided to water the plants on the balcony next to her bedroom - she felt dead, but at least she could keep her plants alive. After filling a plastic pitcher in the kitchen with water, she walked out onto the balcony. While watering the snowball viburnum, Eric popped into her mind again and she began to cry. She realized that she hadn't brought any tissues to blow her nose with and without caring about how revolting it was, used the hem of her shirt. At that moment, she heard someone behind her in a friendly, upbeat voice say, "Hello."

Jessica turned around, half-dazed and mortified to see a good-looking man in his twenties, wearing a navy suit standing on the adjacent balcony, grinning at her. Embarrassed, she politely said, "Hello. Excuse me. Wait just one minute." Hoping that the man hadn't seen what she'd done to her shirt, she hopped back into her bedroom to neaten her appearance. When she returned, he was still there.

"Where's Eric?" he asked.

Jessica wasn't surprised that the man asked a question about Eric – he was much more social than she was with their neighbors. "Eric no longer lives here. We've broken up," she said, bluntly.

A surprised expression crossed his face. "I'm sorry to hear that. I'm Steve, by the way," he said, leaning across his balcony, extending his hand to introduce himself formally.

Jessica shook his hand weakly and was taken aback when he said, "I'd catch him having a smoke out here in the morning sometimes. I see you don't smoke. I've made some coffee. Would you like some?"

Jessica, who viewed any friend of Eric's as an enemy that morning didn't answer. Instead, she paused and looked down at her plants. Steve read her negative body language immediately. "I'm sorry I asked. Maybe you don't drink coffee. Or, you're not in a social mood. If you change your mind, you could just hop over.

We're attached as you can see," he said, pointing to the mid-section of their balconies.

"Maybe later in the week. I'm not really myself today," Jessica said, realizing that she was being rude.

"Understood," Steve replied. "If you ever need anything, I'm right next door. Feel free to give me a shout."

Jessica nodded and then walked back into her bedroom. Taking a seat on the bed, she wondered if she had ever seen Steve before and concluded that she would have remembered meeting a man as attractive as him. This meant that he must have moved into the building recently. Clearly, he liked Eric. But then, everyone liked Eric.

Two days after the breakup, Jessica pulled herself together and went to work. Everyone at the office kept their distance, assuming she was sick. Noticing this, she told her colleagues that her cold was going away, and chose to tell no one about the breakup. Although she worked at a slow pace, something others took notice of, she was able to complete her work.

As the days passed and the initial shock of Eric's rejection wore off, Jessica got used to being home alone in her apartment. Weekends were difficult for her to get through, however. In the middle of the night sometimes she would awaken, believing that she heard Eric rummaging around the kitchen or shutting the bathroom door. When these hallucinations occurred, it was difficult for her to get back to sleep. Sometimes, she would even call out his name, but then reality would set in. "I think I'm going insane," she would whisper in the dark.

A month after the breakup, Eric began sending Jessica chat messages on her cellphone, claiming that he was concerned about her well-being. This made Jessica hopeful that he wanted to get back together. But every time she asked him to come over or meet someplace for dinner, he declined, telling her that he was busy. Questions remained unanswered, the main one being whether he'd left her for another woman. Eric refused to give her definitive answers to any her questions, most of all, that one. He would simply reply: *I'm not in a relationship with anyone else.*

After every one of her conversations with Eric, Jessica became severely depressed. One day, after two weeks of responding to his messages and telling him how much she missed him, she called him and asked in a direct way if he was coming back. "I miss you," Eric said. "But I'm not trying to get back together with you. I just want to know how you are."

Tired by what she considered Eric's shenanigans, and angry at herself for letting him play mind games with her, Jessica told him that she wanted the key back to her apartment. Eric didn't argue and said that he would give it back to her whenever she wanted. They agreed that he would pick up the rest of his things that week when she was at work, and he would leave the key on the entrance table. Not knowing the exact day he would leave the key was better for her emotional state, Jessica felt. Coming home to find it meant that there was no going back. Knowing how devastated she would feel, she asked friends to meet her after work at a pub one block from her apartment that whole week, dreading the moment when she'd find it.

The night she came home to find Eric's key, Jessica was so distraught that she was unable to get even one hour of sleep. The next day she showed up at work, but sat slumped over her desk. She was exhausted both physically and emotionally, but forced herself to continue as if nothing had happened. By the middle of the day however, she began to cave. During an important meeting, she suddenly felt overcome with emotion. After politely excusing herself, she ran to the bathroom and leaned up against one of the stalls, crying uncontrollably. Caroline, a co-worker attending the same meeting, ran after her. Witnessing Jessica's meltdown, she gave her a hug. "You haven't talked about Eric in a long time. We guessed that maybe you broke up, but we thought it was best to let you tell us in your own time. Is it over between you two?" she asked.

Jessica, who had no idea that her co-workers had noticed that something was wrong, nodded and simply said, "Yes."

After having a long talk with Caroline, Jessica felt greatly relieved. She was embarrassed that she had made a scene at work and that everyone had guessed correctly – that she was going through a breakup, but was grateful that they chose to be sympathetic and kind. Outside of work, she had a small group of friends who spent evenings with her trying to cheer her up, taking her out to dinner and going to local hotspots that they knew Eric didn't frequent. A tall, slim, honey-blonde, Jessica always attracted attention from men whenever she went out with her friends. However, after having been in a relationship for so long, she wasn't sure how to respond. She wasn't ready to date again and sometimes felt overwhelmed rather than flattered. Jessica also enjoyed doing activities by herself, one of them being visiting the many galleries and museums located around London. Having begun college as an art major, she'd ended up studying business and followed that career path, but her interest in art remained strong. Eric had never taken an interest in art at all, so she'd usually gone alone to exhibits during their relationship.

Jessica began to spend Saturday afternoons visiting the Tate Gallery, The Victoria and Albert Museum, and the British Museum. She delighted in viewing all the wonderful paintings, Roman sculptures, statues of Egyptian gods, and Greek pottery. After these leisurely outings, she would stop by her favorite café on the way home and have a fabulous dinner. Since she no longer had to be home at a certain hour, she didn't feel rushed and could truly enjoy herself.

After several more weeks of trying her best to recover from the breakup, Jessica finally reached a stage where she no longer needed to have people around her constantly for support. She began putting more energy into her work and slept early. Once she was back on track and on her normal schedule, she started to notice men again. There were two new employees working at her office who she found attractive, but she avoided flirting with them, deeming it inappropriate. Another month went by before she remembered meeting Steve, the good-looking man who lived next door. She fantasized about bumping into him in the hallway of her building and flirting with him shamelessly. The fact that he lived so close bothered her somewhat - what if she tried to seduce him and he turned out to be nuts? Or, what if she hit on him and he rejected her? It would be an awkward situation if she saw him standing on his balcony again. But after giving it some more thought, she decided that it couldn't hurt to be friendly to a neighbor, and whatever the outcome, so be it.

Jessica began to peer through her bedroom window onto Steve's balcony each morning, but he was never there. Wracking her brain, she tried to recall the exact time of day she had spotted him. And then she remembered - it was the morning after Eric left, at 9 a.m. Because she usually left for work at 8:30, it was likely that she would continue to miss seeing him.

Determined to see Steve again, Jessica made an excuse to come to the office late one Monday morning, claiming to have a dental appointment. She woke up an hour later than usual and peered out of her window at exactly 9 a.m. As luck would have it, there he was, joking and laughing with another man. This time she was going to look nice, she decided. She put on a tight floral dress she'd worn to the office a few times with a jacket over it, but left off the jacket so that Steve could see her figure. She quickly pulled on some tights and boots to keep warm, and fixed her makeup and hair. Grabbing her water pitcher, she walked out onto the balcony, and immediately heard Steve exclaim, "There you are. I was thinking about leaving a note on your door ages ago, but I didn't want to seem too forward."

"I've been working a lot lately," Jessica said, noticing that the man standing next to him was also attractive. He smiled and introduced himself as Alistair.

Jessica and Steve stood outside on their adjoined balconies, chatting for over an hour while Alistair paced in the background, walking in and out of Steve's apartment, having an intense, animated conversation on his cellphone. Steve explained that he had recently started a small business, and Alistair was his partner. He said that he usually left for work at 10 a.m. and got

137

home sometimes as late as 10 p.m. Jessica found it interesting that he'd volunteered the details of his schedule because she hadn't asked him about it.

Once Alistair was off the phone, he suggested that Steve invite Jessica to have dinner with them and a group of their friends over the coming weekend. Steve agreed that it was a great idea and took Jessica's number. Jessica, worried that since she wouldn't know anyone, she might feel left out, asked if she could bring her friends, Monica and Kelly along. Alistair's eyes brightened at the suggestion. "You can bring as many women as you'd like," he said.

"Great. It was nice to meet you, Alistair. And Steve, give me a call on Friday to let me know the exact time everyone's meeting up, and we'll drop by," she said.

On Friday night, Jessica and her friends met up with Steve and his friends at an Italian restaurant. They were a lively, friendly group of people, and Jessica enjoyed meeting everyone. When she got home, she looked at her cellphone and saw that it was 2 a.m. She hadn't planned on getting home so late and was surprised at how quickly the evening had flown by. She had spent most of it flirting with Steve.

Steve sent Jessica a chat message two days later, asking her if she had any free time over the next weekend, and if so, he wanted to know if she would have dinner with him, but alone this time. He then suggested that she hop over onto his balcony once in awhile. She messaged him back, telling him that he was welcome to hop over onto her side if he was brave enough, but that the thought of dropping three floors was enough to keep her on her own side. He messaged back that she was worth the risk.

Jessica and Steve began seeing each other and soon it became clear that there was a deep connection between them. Jessica felt incredibly lucky to have met a man she was crazy about so quickly after coming out of a four-year relationship. Both she and Steve began to make changes to their schedules so that they could spend more time together

Jessica is still dating Steve and things are getting more serious, but neither wants to give up their apartment just yet. Steve continues his balcony hopping, and Jessica keeps begging him to use the front door.

Katrina's Breakup

Katrina, a thirty-six-year-old makeup artist, had moved to New York City at the age of twenty from Wisconsin. The chaotic, bustling city that had left her feeling overwhelmed in her twenties now energized her. At the start of her career she had worked with fashion photographers, but after a well-known photographer made inappropriate advances, she tired of the jaded people she met in that industry and took a job at Laurent Cosmetics, an international company. She found the corporate structure and its hierarchy to be formal and sterile at times; the carefully worded emails they sent her were full of legal mumbo-jumbo. However, she felt respected in that environment.

In the sixteen years Katrina lived in Manhattan, she had joined various dating sites and had been on so many dates that she'd lost count. She'd had three serious relationships, but none had worked out in the long run, so she had never married. In the building where she lived were many unmarried women who had interesting social lives and traveled frequently. Becoming friendly with them helped her realize that she was in good company. Resigned to being single, she chose not to put pressure on herself to continue actively dating. She felt that it would be nice to have romance again in her life, but she accepted things as they were.

Katrina had a small group of friends that she got together with in her spare time. But it wasn't easy for everyone to juggle their schedules, so she found herself alone much of the time. Not a fan of social media, she maintained only one account, directly related to her work. Through this account she would receive announcements and information regarding off-site training. One evening, after a long day of discussing the company's line of foundations and bb creams with a group of new salespeople, Katrina came home to her apartment to find that she had left her laptop on all day. It sat open on an antique desk she had recently bought at auction. She'd left the window open in the kitchen and rain had fallen on both the laptop and desk. After shutting the window, grabbing some paper towels, and wiping everything down, she took a seat and checked to see if her laptop had been damaged. Luckily, no water had gotten inside, so she directed her attention to her social media page and read some work announcements. That's when she noticed another message that didn't pertain to work. It read: *Hello Kat. It's Simon. How are you these days?*

Confused, Katrina removed her coat and placed it on the back of her chair. After reading the message twice more, it finally registered with her – it was from Simon Leroux, a European man she had dated over twelve years ago at the age of twenty-four. It had to be him because she knew no other Simon. She was flattered that he remembered her, but was surprised that he had reached out to her in this way.

Katrina's relationship with Simon had lasted for six months but faded into history following the pattern of her early romances when she was finding her own identity. Simon had been only twenty-one-years-old when they'd dated, a fact that she felt had ultimately doomed their relationship. Leaning back against her coat and crossing her legs, she recalled some of the romantic moments they had shared. A memory she'd carried with her over the years still stood out inexplicably in her mind, as clear as if it had happened yesterday. One morning, after having spent the night with Simon at his apartment, she awoke to find him standing over her. As she opened her eyes, she looked up at him and thought that he resembled a statue of Adonis she had seen in a Greek history book at the library. He was tall with a lean, muscular frame. His glossy brown hair was thick and wavy, and his facial features looked like they had been sculpted by an artist. There was no denying that his looks are what had won Katrina over when he'd hit on her at the gym. If the profile photo that popped up alongside his message represented him accurately, he looked pretty much the same.

Katrina continued to stare at the computer screen, dreaming about the Simon she once knew. She still remembered the scent of his cologne; she had even bought herself a bottle from a department store at the beginning of their relationship because it reminded her of him and made her feel like he was always near. She recalled what it was like to sleep next to him, her head on his chest, and the warmth of his body. But when she thought more about her past with him, she was also reminded of some of the things that she disliked. Simon rarely showed emotion, something that used to make her feel lonely. His robotic behavior was so off-putting at times that it didn't matter how gorgeous he was. He wasn't argumentative, which was a plus in her book, but his personality was so flat that he was almost dull. He hardly ever cracked a joke, and when Katrina told a funny story, he had difficulty processing the punchline. He had a stiff demeanor, comparable to a stereotypical British butler represented in BBC period pieces. Simon's lackadaisical personality sometimes gave her the sense that he was limited intellectually even though she knew that wasn't the case. He had a high IQ and excelled in math and science in college, something that had made her proud of him.

Simon would often compliment Katrina's appearance, telling her how beautiful she was which gave her an ego boost. But while she enjoyed the attention and compliments, she suspected that he was objectifying her. Apparently aware of his inability to impress her with conversation, he created a situation where their relationship turned purely sexual. Her new friend at the time, Alexis, also a makeup artist who she'd met while working in the fashion industry, felt that their age difference was to blame for his lack of conversational skills. Katrina vividly recalled something Alexis had said about Simon while jogging next to her in Central Park, all those years ago. "What do you expect from this scary-good-looking twenty-one-year-old French kid? He wants to sleep with you and that's his main focus. If you feel that he's connecting with you physically but not mentally, you should date other people. Anyway, you haven't been together long."

Katrina agreed with her friend that Simon was undeveloped. Nevertheless, she was ambivalent to break up with him or go on dates with other men. She had developed feelings for him and felt a strong "chemical attachment," a term she'd coined from Alexis. Confused about what to do, Katrina began to spend less time with Simon so that she could gain a better understanding of her feelings. She stopped instigating contact with him, but took his calls and continued to be intimate with him. One evening, when she was in bed reading a book, he called her after midnight, and asked, "Are you trying to break up with me?"

Katrina knew that eventually he would conclude that something was wrong, but she needed to buy more time to figure out if she wanted to continue seeing him. "Absolutely not," she said. Removing her glasses, she fluffed up her pillow and sat back against it. "I'd like to work on our relationship and make sure that we have enough in common. There seems to be something missing."

"I didn't know that we didn't have enough in common. This is the first time you've said anything to me," said Simon, quietly.

Katrina changed the subject by asking him about a math test he had taken that week. But Simon's disappointed tone of voice didn't change during the rest of their conversation, and she knew that she'd hurt his feelings.

A few days after their conversation, Katrina began to feel that she had made a mistake by pulling away from Simon. But when she rang his number, to her surprise, he didn't answer. After a week of not hearing from him and knowing that he must have seen her missed call, she began to miss him badly and called him again, but this time his number was disconnected. Confused and panicked, she went to his apartment. Everett, his doorman recognized her and stopped her as she stood in front the elevator to tell her that he had moved out. According to him, Simon told his landlord that his father had died and that he was moving back to France to be with his family. Stunned by the news, Katrina was upset that he had never called her to tell her that he was leaving or allow her to console him after the death of his father. Believing that she had lost him because of her callous behavior, she cried so hard that she could barely make the walk back home to her tiny studio apartment. She suffered depression for weeks, and struggled to get herself up in the mornings and go to work. Eventually, she began dating again, but she always felt badly about the ending of her relationship with Simon. Now, twelve years later, he was reaching out to her. She had no idea why, but she saw it as an opportunity to renew a friendship and apologize for how she behaved in the past. Katrina responded politely to Simon's message: *I'm doing well. Thanks for asking. How are you? And, where are you?*

Simon wrote back within seconds: *I'm a commercial pilot for Air France. I'm in Paris.*

Katrina remembered that Simon had always wanted to be a pilot. She was happy for him that he had pursued his dream. Katrina wrote: *Paris is a beautiful city. I'm still in NYC.*

Simon replied: *I'll be in NYC in a week and I'll be staying for two days. Can I see you? Your relationship status says "single."*

Deciding to maintain a casual tone, Katrina wrote: *Yes, of course. Message me when you're here and we'll meet up.*

When Simon didn't respond, Katrina assumed that their conversation was over and switched off her laptop. She made her way to the bedroom to change out of her work clothes. Removing her blouse and skirt, she threw them on the bed along with her cellphone and then stepped out of her heels. Still thinking about Simon, she hoped that his job as a pilot had changed him. Traveling the world often made people more interesting and sophisticated – she wondered if that would be the case with him. As she searched through her closet for a tank top, her cellphone began whistling. She picked it up, opened the app that had sent her the notification, and saw that Simon had responded to her last message by giving her his phone number. Confused by his persistence, she sat down on the bed and tried to collect her thoughts. Simon would be thirty-three-years-old now, she guessed. Assuming that pilots were surrounded by beautiful young stewardesses, she wondered why he had bothered contacting her. "Maybe he's had his share of failed relationships with co-workers," she said to herself, pulling a blue tank top over hear head. Deciding not to overthink the situation, she concluded that Simon probably no longer knew anyone in New York and just wanted a dinner companion.

On a Sunday morning, nearly a week after her chat with Simon on social media, Katrina's cellphone began whistling. Awoken from a dream, her eyes still closed, she felt around the bedside table searching for it until she grasped it. Opening her eyes, she looked at the phone - the bright glare of the screen caused her to wince as she read a message from Simon. He wrote that he was staying at a hotel for two days near the JFK Airport, and that he wanted to meet her for lunch if she didn't have any plans. Looking at the time on her phone she saw that it was just after 9 a.m. She wrote back: *Meet me at 1:00 at Claire's Cafe on 56th Street. There's only one Claire's in Manhattan, so you should find it easily.*

Simon responded: *See you then.*

At 12:55 that afternoon, Katrina left her apartment and walked down the street to Claire's Café, a place she had chosen for its European charm. Once she arrived, she looked at the people sitting at the rows of tables outside but didn't see a man that resembled her old friend. Simon had always been on time in his youth, so she assumed that he was inside the restaurant, already waiting for her. The moment she reached the entrance and grasped the door handle she heard a familiar voice call her name from behind. Turning around, she saw a tall handsome man in an expensive-looking blazer and dark jeans closing the back door of a car and walking towards her - she immediately recognized him as Simon. As he reached the pavement and came closer, she saw that he had lost the baby-fat in his face and had more chiseled features, making him even more gorgeous than in his twenties. Looking at the perfection of his jaw line, she noticed five o'clock shadow which gave him a lazy, yet sexy appearance. She wondered how he had recognized her in her large black sunglasses, but then realized that her figure hadn't changed much, and she was back to wearing the same hairstyle she had worn in her twenties; her long,

146

espresso-brown hair hung just past her shoulders and was styled to hang straight. "Simon, it's wonderful to see you," she said, walking towards him. They gave each other a quick hug and Katrina took in the scent of his cologne. It was modern and sporty, totally different than the scent he had worn in his youth.

A hostess walked outside to greet them and asked them where they wanted to sit. Since it was a beautiful sunny day, they decided to sit outside next to an enormous pot of blue and pink flowers. "Hydrangeas are your favorite. I remember that," said Simon, taking a seat.

"Actually, it's peonies, but hydrangeas are a close second," Katrina said, smoothing the back of her dress as she sat down. Simon's French accent was much lighter than it used to be; she guessed that it was due to the fact that English was the mandated international language of aviation, so he likely spoke it every day.

"You look beautiful. I was so in love with you all those years ago. Now I know why."

Katrina removed her designer sunglasses and slipped them into her handbag. "I've held up pretty well, I suppose. You look better than me," she said.

"How have you been?" he asked, looking down at the table, embarrassed by her compliment.

"I'm fine. I missed you all those years ago when you disappeared. I went looking for you at your apartment, but you weren't there."

Simon shifted in his chair uncomfortably, as if he didn't want to discuss that aspect of their past. "My father died of a heart attack. I thought it best to go back to France. I'm an only child."

"Your doorman, Everett informed me," said Katrina. "You never said that you were leaving. You just vanished. I missed your company."

"But I was awkward," said Simon, bluntly.

"A bit," said Katrina, biting her lower lip, pained by Simon's unexpected admission.

"Did you know that I was a virgin? You were my first love. I was so happy to have found you. But you didn't have the same feelings for me as I had for you."

"I had no idea," said Katrina, having guessed that to be the case.

"You were dating other people back then, weren't you?"

Katrina paused – it had never occurred to her that Simon would have suspected her of cheating. "Absolutely not. I never dated anyone else while I was seeing you. But I think that the age difference between us was a problem. Obviously, it wouldn't be now."

Water was brought to their table and soon after, a waiter arrived to take their order. After he walked away, Simon stared at the glass in front of him. Katrina tried to read his facial expression and thought that he looked sad. Just as she was about to ask him if he was feeling alright, he looked at her suddenly, a broad grin on his face. To Katrina, he looked like a male model in a toothpaste advertisement. "We can start fresh. Forget about the past. We know each other again. That's what matters."

"I'm so glad you contacted me," said Katrina. She wondered why he was showing romantic interest in her so quickly and made the assumption that he had just come out of a relationship.

148

"I think we'll have more in common now. I've seen the world, and I'm sophisticated enough to converse with an 'older woman'," he said, winking.

Katrina rolled her eyes and laughed. "Thanks for rubbing it in."

"Obviously, it's irrelevant," he said.

"You never married?" Katrina asked.

"I've been in two serious relationships. One woman I met in England where I was training. We were engaged but broke up several years ago. And recently I was in a long-term relationship with a colleague, but that also ended."

Katrina was relieved that he had volunteered the most important aspects of his dating history, rather than making her drop subtle hints to try and pull it out of him. "And you thought of contacting me?" she said, dropping the words casually.

"You've been on my mind all these years."

"Why is that?"

"For some reason, I have a tendency to compare every woman I date to you. The memory of our time together has haunted me, but in a good way," he said.

Katrina looked over at him calmly, trying her best not to show him how excited she was at the prospect of dating him again. "I see."

"New York is on my roster now, so I'll be flying here every other week. I have more flexibility than I used to, now that I've been with the airline for a few years. I can continue to request that New York remain on my roster. Would you like me to do that?"

"Sure. We can meet up again," said Katrina.

"That's the plan," said Simon, smiling.

Katrina was impressed with Simon's newfound ability to make light conversation and felt a strong romantic spark. She had recently decided to take a break from dating due to burnout. Meeting new men constantly and not finding someone she felt was the right match for her had taken its toll, causing her to feel exhausted, but not hopeless – not yet anyway. Simon wasn't someone she knew absolutely nothing about like the other men, and the familiarity was comforting. Relaxed in his company, Katrina decided to turn on her feminine charms. Leaning against the table, flashing just enough cleavage to gain his attention, a subtle smile crossed her lips. Just as she was about to speak, Simon cut her off. "Did I mention how much I liked your dress?"

After her date with Simon, Katrina began walking home in a daze, completely unaware that her cellphone was ringing. Finally, noticing that the loud tune she heard was coming from her own handbag, she clumsily fumbled around inside it, grabbed her phone, and saw that her best friend, Alexis was attempting to start a Skype conversation. Katrina accepted the call, put the speakerphone on, and raised the volume. "I'm on the street walking home. You'll have to speak loudly," said Katrina, picking up her pace, hoping to reach her apartment building quickly so that she could speak to her friend in a less noisy environment.

"Aren't you coming over today? Remember, you were supposed to help me choose a paint color for the living room?" said Alexis. She opened the video on her phone and placed it in front of a set of paint swatches.

Katrina stopped walking and stood still in the middle of the sidewalk so that she could look carefully at the swatches. "I like the aqua," she said.

"Really? I was thinking that the British racing green would be classier."

"Your apartment is small. A green that dark will make it feel even smaller. You need to brighten it up," she said. "By the way, you're not going to believe who I just had lunch with."

"Who?" said Alexis, turning the video-mode off.

"Remember Simon, that gorgeous guy I dated over a decade ago - the one who went back to France?" Katrina said.

Alexis popped open a bottle of Pellegrino and took a seat on the sofa. "How could I forget him? He was madly in love with you and incredibly good-looking. But I seriously contemplated asking him to show me his ID when I met him. I thought he looked younger than what he claimed to be. And I remember you telling me that he acted like a butler, and all he wanted to do was have sex."

"That's the one!" exclaimed Katrina. "He contacted me on social media and asked me to meet up with him. He's a commercial pilot now and flies to New York. I think he wants me back."

"He calls you after all these years and asks you to meet up with him, and just like that, you're together again? I hate to burst your bubble, but half of my ex-boyfriends have contacted me on social media, and most of them are married, so I just ignore them now. There's no reason to revisit a failed relationship."

Hearing her friend's opinion was important to Katrina because Alexis often gave her good advice. She slowed her pace so that she could concentrate and explain the situation better. "My intention was just to catch up with an old friend who was in town. But, I felt a spark at lunch and I haven't felt that way in a long time. He's even more gorgeous now than he was then, and he's wittier and a hundred times more charming. It's as if he's had a lobotomy."

Alexis laughed. "That's wonderful – he needed one. But he's a commercial pilot who flies all over the world in a small space with beautiful stewardesses. I'd never date a pilot."

Katrina felt a sudden queasiness in the pit of her stomach. "I was thinking that the other day. If I were a young stewardess working with a pilot that attractive, I'd probably try to get his attention."

"That's exactly my point, but I wasn't trying to be negative. It's just something that came to mind," said Alexis. "My friend Lilly's husband is a pilot and he's never cheated on her. They've been married for twenty years. Also, I have a friend who was a stewardess in the first class cabin a few years ago. She's dated a plastic surgeon, a diplomat, and a polo player, but never a pilot."

"How comforting," said Katrina, her happy-bubble burst.

Not wanting to put her friend in a pessimistic state of mind, Alexis changed the subject. "You've already had lunch, but I'm starving, so I'll order some pasta from the restaurant downstairs. When are you coming by?"

Katrina finally reached her building and stepped inside the lobby. "I'll change now and come right over," she said. Catching her breath after the long walk, she stepped onto the elevator. Pressing the button to her floor, she wondered if Simon had women in different cities, all over the world. It was possible that he was simply adding her to his list.

* * *

Katrina and Simon began spending time together whenever he flew into JFK, and soon a relationship developed. They maintained regular contact in between by chat messaging or calling each other. If these conversations took place in the evening when Katrina was home, Simon would always insist that she open the video on her phone or laptop so that he could see her while speaking with her. Katrina, thrilled to be back together with the new suave Simon, wanted to maintain his interest, so she did as he asked without argument. She would accept his call, apply a bit of makeup, and then find an area of her apartment that had the best lighting before opening the video-mode on her phone. This was a chore, but if it made him happy, that's all that mattered to Katrina. Within a few weeks, Katrina felt like she was falling in love with Simon. Normally, she would have never allowed herself to become vulnerable so soon, but her history with him made her feel at ease.

After several months of meeting Simon regularly for a passionate rendezvous whenever he was in town, on a Saturday afternoon, he called Katrina from Frankfurt and told her that he could no longer keep New York on his roster, but that he would try to regain the route again in a year. "A year?" said Katrina, disappointed. "You can't trade with another pilot? I don't exactly know how the scheduling works, but you told me you'd worked for the same airline a number of years."

"Unfortunately, I don't have the type of seniority necessary to maintain that route any longer. I thought I did, but that turned out not to be the case," he said.

"When will we see each other again?"

"You could meet me in London once or twice a month," he said. "It's a reasonably short flight from New York. I stay there a couple of days every fortnight now, instead. I can tell you which days ahead of time so that we can synchronize our schedules. I'm also planning a vacation in six months. I can come to you, or we can take a trip somewhere, if you'd like."

"I suppose we could work it out," said Katrina, walking from the kitchen to the bedroom. Taking a seat on the bed, she waited for him to tell her something that would make her feel more secure about the direction of their relationship.

"Don't worry about it now, Katrina. Let me get accustomed to my new schedule and then we can make a plan to meet up. I've got to go, sweetheart. I'll call you from Paris," he said, ending the call.

Less than a minute after she hung up the call with Simon, Katrina's cellphone rang again. She prayed that it was Simon calling her back to tell her that he was mistaken and that he would be able maintain his same schedule. Anxiously, she looked at her phone and saw that it was Alexis. Normally, when Alexis called, Katrina said an upbeat hello to her. But this time she said nothing and waited for her friend to speak first. This caused Alexis to suspect that something was wrong. "What's going on?" she asked, concerned.

Katrina rose from the bed and began pacing. "Simon's schedule has changed. New York is no longer on his roster."

"That's too bad. I was wondering when his roster would change but I didn't want to say anything to you about it."

"Do you think that I should ask someone in human resources if I can move to London or even better, Paris? Then, I could be with him all the time."

"You could do that, I guess. Your company has stores in both cities and you have years of experience. But if you move to Paris you'll have to learn French."

Katrina had thought of that issue herself, but felt it was a moot point at that moment. "The main problem is this - for all I know his schedule could change again, and instead of Europe, he could end up flying to Bangkok and Viet Nam," she said.

"That's what I was thinking too. If I were you I'd sit tight and maybe get a hobby to keep myself busy until I got a feel for where my relationship was headed," Alexis said.

"I'm so disappointed. I love Simon. What we have between us is amazing, and we have a history together which makes it even more special. But when I spoke with him just now, he almost sounded like he didn't care that he wouldn't be seeing me regularly anymore."

"I'm sure he cares. But since he couldn't change anything, he felt it best to accept the situation."

"Maybe you're right," said Katrina. "Do you want to go for a jog in the park? It's still early evening."

"Sure, I can be at your place in half an hour."

Katrina changed into a track suit, grabbed a bottle of water, and walked downstairs to the lobby of her building. Feeling suddenly tired, she wasn't sure that she was still in the mood to go jogging. But one thing was certain – it was better than sitting home alone, obsessing about Simon.

* * *

A week passed before Simon sent Katrina a chat message asking her if she was available to talk to him on video. When she saw the message on her phone she had just gotten home from work and was disheveled. She left her coat on a hook at the entrance, and after fixing her makeup quickly, she took a seat on the sofa where the lighting was best at that hour. Tapping on the video option, she saw Simon's handsome face looking back at her.

"Hi gorgeous," said Simon. He was holding his phone at arms length, allowing Katrina to see that he was sitting on a king-size bed in a hotel room.

"Are you watching t.v.?" she asked.

Simon panned around the room with his phone so that she could see what his room looked like and then back again. "Not really. It's just background noise."

The duvet cover of the bed he sat on was ivory, and she noticed a black rectangular object next to his other hand. "Is that the remote?" she asked, squinting. And then she heard it ring.

"No," said Simon. "That's my other phone. I bought it a few days ago. Wait one minute. Someone's calling me."

"You can call me back if you'd like," said Katrina, not wanting to keep him from an important call.

Simon gestured that the call would take only one minute. He then picked up the other phone and placed it to his ear. While speaking, he continued holding up the phone in his left hand so that Katrina could see him in profile. She watched him smiling and then laughing as if he had just heard a hysterical joke, a reaction she'd never seen from him. Still holding both phones, he turned his head to look at Katrina. "Are most American women overweight?" Simon asked.

Startled by a question that sounded like an insulting dig directed at her, Katrina said, "There are a variety of people in the U.S. Some are thin, and some are overweight. But if you're talking about obesity, it's a global problem. Are you suggesting that I'm fat? I'm probably underweight for my height."

Simon spoke in hushed tones into the other phone and then a serious expression crossed his face. Once he ended the call, he placed the phone back down on the bed. Looking at Katrina once again he said, "I'm sorry about that. Of course, you're not overweight. You have a beautiful figure. It was a rude question."

"What was that about?"

Simon took in a deep breath and exhaled. "You know that I meet a lot of women in my line of work."

"Yes. I'm sure you do," she said, already concerned about where their conversation was headed.

"This girl I was speaking with…she works at the Charles de Gaul Airport."

Katrina, considered by her friends to be a battle-hardened Manhattan dating expert, knew immediately that she had aggressive competition. Practiced at keeping her cool she maintained a casual tone. "And she has your new number?"

"She needs it for security purposes," he said, as if the fact should have been obvious.

"Why did you get a second phone?"

"I upgraded the phone I'm speaking with you on, and they gave me a deal on a second one, so I bought both. Also, I like having two phones," he said, turning his head towards the television mounted on the wall. Simon usually looked directly at Katrina whenever he spoke to her. And the fact that he was unable to speak face-to-face was a red flag. Katrina knew instantly that the woman on the phone with Simon had pressured him into poking fun at her, and that he now felt ashamed that he'd gone along with it.

"Are you dating her?" Katrina asked.

The shock of the question caused Simon to wince. He turned to look at her. "I consider her a friend. Admittedly, the girl is pretty, but she's young. She has a flirtatious personality and she follows me around."

"And you like the attention."

"Let's change the subject," said Simon.

After her conversation with Simon ended, Katrina removed her ankle boots and laid back on the sofa. Looking up at the ceiling, she tried to connect the dots and figure out what exactly was going on with Simon. She knew that an attractive young woman was chasing him and had his new phone number. She could see that the girl was calling and chatting with him regularly, just as she was doing, but on his other phone. Obviously, what had begun as a flirtation in a work setting had developed into something more. Katrina also gathered that Simon had told the girl that he was in a relationship with an American, and that she was upset about it. Simon obviously felt flattered by her attention but was not particularly interested in her. However, she was trying desperately to get him, and she had a shot at it clearly, judging by the smile on his face when he spoke with her. Katrina suspected that she would continue to throw herself at Simon until he finally gave in, and there was nothing she could do about it.

Guessing that she had been lying on the sofa for over an hour, Katrina sat finally up. Convinced that she was going to have a panic attack, she called Alexis, who thankfully, answered. Stumbling over her words, Katrina explained to her in detail what had occurred, hoping that she would tell her that she was jumping to the wrong conclusions. But instead, Alexis validated in her concerns. When Alexis became nervous, she had an irritating habit of clicking her tongue. This usually annoyed Katrina, but today it had a calming effect on her. It meant that her friend was empathizing with her, something she desperately needed. "Can I drop by?" asked Katrina. "I need help with this."

"You can if you want to, but I'm with Caleb. We were just about to go to dinner. You can come with us," she said.

"I don't want to intrude on your evening out with your boyfriend," said Katrina, quietly, a tear falling down her cheek. "Go to dinner and have a nice time. I can ring you tomorrow."

"I'm not sure that it's a good idea for you to be alone. You sound like you're starting to crumble," said Alexis.

"I'm upset, but I'll deal with it. I'll get through tonight okay. Nobody died." Just as Katrina was about to end the call, she heard a man's voice on the other end.

"Hi Katrina. It's Caleb. Alex had you on speakerphone and I overheard your problem."

"Alexis, why didn't you tell me? I'm so embarrassed," said Katrina, annoyed.

"Listen, Kat, let me be honest with you," Caleb said. "You know that I work in advertising at a large firm. Over the years, several young female interns have aggressively come on to me. I've even talked to Alex about it. Yes, many were very attractive and intelligent. But I prefer women closer to my age, and even older because I like the fact that most are confident, well-rounded, and good conversationalists. Very young women rarely have that sort of sophistication – it develops over time. From what Alex told me, this pilot you're seeing has the same preferences."

"Thank you for trying to cheer me up, but I'm pretty sure that my boyfriend is either sleeping with this person or will be soon," Katrina said, grabbing a tissue and blotting her eyes. She studied the black mascara blotches on it that reminded her of a Rorschach test before blowing her nose into it.

"Let me get to the main point then, and maybe you'll feel better. If Simon begins seeing this girl, it will end. He won't stay with her."

"But he'll likely be seduced by her," said Katrina, blowing her nose again.

"I don't know him, so I can't make a judgment call on that," he said. "But I'm one hundred percent certain that if he ends up seeing her behind your back that he'll come back to you. Although you feel helpless now, you're in the power position in the long run."

Katrina grabbed a can of soda off the coffee table and took a sip. It was from the day before and flat, but she continued drinking it anyway. "I understand your logic, but I don't want to be in a relationship with a cheater."

"If you've already decided that you won't take him back if he has a fling with this girl, you can inform him so that he knows whatever decision he makes will have permanent consequences. Or, you can simply write him off," said Caleb. "Alex and I have to leave now because we have reservations. But think about what I said."

"Alright, I will. Thanks, Caleb," said Katrina. Angry at herself for having allowed Simon back into her life in the first place, she threw the now empty can of soda against the wall. "Why didn't I see this coming?" she shouted in frustration.

Katrina felt the need to get her mind off Simon immediately. So, a few days after their video chat she signed up for a makeup training course given on weekends by her company, introducing the latest trends. Even though she had been a makeup artist for years, she remained open to new techniques and ideas. To get to her company's training facility she had to take the subway a long distance which was an inconvenience, but in her state of mind it was a welcome distraction.

Katrina's decision to get further training turned out to be a smart choice. To her surprise, a few days after she began taking the course, she received an email from her company commending her for furthering her knowledge and thanking her for the years she had worked for them. It was indicated towards the end of the last paragraph that she was up for a raise. This was good news for Katrina, whose rent had gone up recently.

While walking towards the subway through the pouring rain on a Saturday morning, three weeks into her training, her cellphone rang. Pulling it out of her tote bag, she saw Simon's name displayed. Standing under a store awning in an attempt to stay dry, she placed her umbrella down on the pavement and accepted the call, putting it on video-mode. Strangely, Simon didn't do the same. "You haven't called me in awhile," said Katrina.

"I'm sorry. I've been getting used to my new schedule," he said.

"I was thinking of shifting to London, but I haven't spoken to HR about it yet. It would be a nice change for me, and I would get to see you," Katrina said. Hearing no response from Simon, she began to wonder whether he had heard her, when he finally spoke.

"I didn't think you'd make changes in your life to be with me," said Simon. "I don't want you to do that."

"Why not?"

Simon paused before speaking. "Katrina, I didn't want to discuss this now, but since you're considering moving to London, I think I should be honest with you. Remember that girl who rang me on my other phone the last time we spoke?"

"Yes," said Katrina, knowing from experience what she was likely about to hear, and dreading it.

"She's been living with me for a month. She couldn't pay her rent, so she asked if she could stay with me. It will take her awhile to save up enough to move out."

Katrina, feeling that Simon had been easily manipulated, became angry. "You've ditched me for this girl?" she said, making no attempt to hide her hostility.

"Don't take it that way," he said. "At first I was annoyed that I couldn't get rid of her. And then she began to call me all the time. She came over once to give me a jacket that I'd left at the airport and ended up hanging out at my place. Recently, she couldn't pay her rent and ended up here. It just sort of happened."

"I didn't just happen. You've been played, you fool. But there's a price you're going to pay. And that price is losing me," said Katrina, shouting into the phone.

"Please don't say that. I don't know what will happen with this girl. I'm not sure about the future. But please promise me that when I contact you again, you'll take my calls," begged Simon.

Katrina, enraged, laughed sarcastically. "Promise you what? The only thing I'm going to promise you is that you'll never see me or speak with me again in your lifetime. You got that?" After hanging up on him, not wanting to give Simon the option of contacting her again, she stood under the awning, blocking him on the messaging apps they'd used to communicate as well as her social media account. She then looked at the time on her phone, ran down the steps to the subway, and caught it just in time.

During her makeup course that day, Katrina was barely able to concentrate. When she returned home, she finally ate some yogurt and an apple, rested awhile, and afterwards, spent the afternoon cleaning her apartment from top to bottom. That night she struggled to sleep, and at around 5 a.m. she began to cry. She would miss Simon terribly and she knew it. But determined to pull herself through the breakup, she picked up a book, read a couple of chapters, and finally fell back to sleep.

Over the next four months, Katrina had moments when she obsessed about Simon and desperately wanted to speak with him. But she chose to continue blocking him and made no attempt to contact him. Sitting home alone in the evenings, eating dinner by herself and watching movies, she would sometimes wonder about what life was like for him and his new girlfriend. She imagined Simon and a gorgeous young girl making love on a Persian rug inside of an elegant apartment in the heart Paris. It took a great deal of strength for her to snap out of these depressing daydreams when they entered her mind. She saw herself as the reject – the older woman in the scenario - abandoned, alone, and determined to get past the pain. To change her thinking pattern and stay focused on other things, she decided to take an online language course offered for free through her local library. Although she'd always had an interest in French, she chose to learn Italian instead. She also watched cooking shows and tried out new recipes. On Saturdays, she continued to go to off-site training, and every Sunday afternoon, she and Alexis would go for a jog together.

One evening, after work, Katrina's friend Alicia called her while she was preparing dinner. Alicia had thrown a party a week earlier that Katrina didn't attend because she'd been too depressed to socialize. Katrina took the opportunity to explain to her about what had happened with Simon. "I'm feeling a bit better now, but I just can't seem to get past the depression," Katrina said, sitting down at the kitchen table with a plate of couscous.

Alicia told Katrina that she thought she'd handled the breakup well, but she didn't like to see her in a rut. "You told him that you'd never speak to him again and you meant it, so he's a big fat zero in your life. He no longer exists in your world, so wipe his memory from your mind. I think you should date again," she suggested.

"And traumatize myself some more? I'm not strong enough."

"You could always put up a new dating profile online and make it clear that you're looking not only for a romantic partner but a good friend, as well."

"If I do that, no one will contact me," said Katrina, shaking her head.

"Not necessarily. That's how I met my husband. Most of the men who contacted me were only looking at my photos and half of them didn't even read my bio, but Jason did. Jason also wanted a good friend with common interests rather than a hook-up. We spoke on the phone and chat messaged each other for weeks before meeting in person."

After her conversation with Alicia, Katrina finished eating dinner, and afterwards, sat down at her desk in front of her laptop. She searched online to find out which dating sites were trending and came across a new site that interested her. Feeling lazy, she set up a basic profile with three photos and wrote a brief bio about herself. Deciding not to take her plunge into the dating world again too seriously, during the weeks that followed, she checked her email on the website's inbox every three or four days to see if anyone interesting had contacted her. She also began contacting men, feeling that she should be proactive.

Two days after contacting the men on the site, she checked her cellphone during her lunch break and saw that three had responded. One in particular got her attention - his name was Marco. He'd written in his bio that he owned an art gallery and displayed a picture himself standing in front of it. Katrina was familiar with the building – it wasn't far from where she lived. She tapped on the screen of her phone to look at more of his photos and noticed that in all of them he was smiling. His smile appeared genuine because his eyes were smiling too. In each picture he wore a classy-looking suit, and although he appeared to have a muscular frame, he didn't show off his body with shirtless pictures or tank tops like men often did on dating sites which turned her off. He had a well-trimmed beard and mustache, and his hair was dark with a slight streak of gray in the front. His sparkling green eyes complimented his olive complexion. Masculine and aristocratic, he reminded her of a hero in an Italian opera. She messaged him through the site, and was so bold as to write her phone number.

That evening, Marco called Katrina at home. The moment he spoke in his deep, friendly voice, Katrina knew that she wanted to meet him in person. "You have a beautiful accent," she said. "You weren't born here?"

"I'm originally from Argentina. My family moved here when I was nine, so I still have an accent, unfortunately, even though I've tried hard to get rid of it," he said.

"I've walked by your gallery, but I've never gone inside. Did you have a party there two weeks ago? I remember it was crowded and I saw champagne being served."

"Yes, I did. It's a shame you didn't step inside. I would have met you sooner," he replied, smoothly.

Katrina enjoyed her conversation with Marco, but there was one issue that concerned her - she knew little about art and was worried that once they met, they would have nothing to talk about. Nevertheless, she agreed to meet him the next evening for dinner at an Italian restaurant across the street from his gallery. She knew that the next time she spoke with Alicia she would reprimand her for not talking to him longer before meeting him in person. But feeling a pang of optimism, she wanted to get their first date out of the way. When she'd met men online in the past, she developed a momentum because the feeling of constantly moving forward kept her from becoming hurt when she was rejected or disappointed. If things didn't work out with Marco she planned to continue contacting other men and remaining open to the ones who contacted her.

On the night of her date with Marco, Katrina threw on a flattering black dress that she wore frequently, and arrived at the restaurant earlier than she had planned. While standing under the green awning in front of a group of tables already filling up with people, she spotted Marco across the street, inside his brightly lit gallery. After he finished speaking with a woman she guessed was an employee, he walked out the door and stepped onto the street. Once the cars came to a stop at a nearby intersection, Marco ran across the street. As he ran, he looked straight ahead and noticed Katrina. When he reached her he said, "You must be Katrina. I almost got myself killed. You're so beautiful, that I couldn't help but run towards you." A friendly smile on his face, he gave her a gentle hug and a quick kiss on both cheeks. Katrina rolled her eyes at the over-the-top compliment, but hugged him back.

During dinner, Marco was lively and brimmed with positive energy, the complete opposite of Simon. He'd had a difficult but interesting life and spoke about his experiences in an open and honest way, leading Katrina to believe that he took things with ease and wasn't ruled by his ego. Once the profiteroles she ordered for dessert arrived, she asked him about his favorite artists. Marco dropped several names and gave her detailed explanations as to why he thought their work was either brilliant or unusual. Wanting to better understand Marco's world, Katrina tried to remember some of the names he mentioned so that she could look them up online.

After Marco paid the bill, Katrina told him that she had to go home because she had to be at work early the next morning. Marco smiled and nodded that he understood, and suggested that they meet again over the weekend. Katrina, relieved that he'd asked her on a second date already, told him that she would be delighted to meet him again. When he said goodbye, he hugged her and kissed her on both cheeks again as if she were an old friend before making his way back across the street to his gallery.

Katrina and Marco began seeing each other and a romantic relationship developed. In his company, she felt at peace with herself and the world. He wasn't judgmental or shallow, and she sensed that he cared for her, and was trying his best to get to know her. One evening, lying on Marco's chest in his bed, she admitted to him that she'd been studying the artists he mentioned on their first date, but that modern art had never interested her because in her opinion, a lot of it was nonsense. "I'm not at all offended by what you're saying. Art goes through different phases, and overall it's in a trashy phase now, meant to evoke shock. But the artists I work with are skilled and their work has true depth and meaning," he said. Pleased that she had taken an interest, he stroked her hair and suggested she

168

come to lunch with him and one of the artists the following week.

Six months into their relationship, Marco introduced Katrina to his family, and by the end of the year, he proposed to her during a stroll in Central Park. She was taken by surprise when he pulled her aside and presented her with a ring. Having fallen in love with him, she said yes.

When Katrina got home that afternoon, she called Alexis to tell her the good news. "I can't believe it. Marco and I are getting married. In over twenty years of dating, not one man has ever proposed," she said, breathlessly.

"That's not true. Don't you remember Stan? And apparently, you've forgotten all about Kevin. Both wanted to settle down with you, but you didn't want to be with them."

"Neither of them actually proposed – they only dropped hints. I meant that it's a miracle, after all these years, that I'm in love with a man who loves me back and wants to marry me," said Katrina.

After a small intimate summer wedding with only their closest friends and family in attendance, Katrina and Marco decided to move into a two-bedroom apartment in her building while they looked for a condominium to buy in a location that suited both their needs. Although Marco earned a good living and could support them both, Katrina wanted to continue working and had no plans to quit being a makeup artist. She insisted that whatever they buy, it had to be within walking distance of her workplace.

Three weeks after their wedding, on a Wednesday morning, Katrina heard the doorbell ring. So as not to wake Marco, she slipped out of bed quietly and answered the door. Looking through the peephole she saw Ron, the doorman holding a huge bouquet of flowers. Pleasantly surprised, she opened the door and looked down at the bouquet. "You didn't answer your phone this morning. It's getting hot and humid already, so I wanted to bring these up to you immediately," he said.

"These are for me? Are you sure?"

"It says your name on the card, but it was being sent to your old apartment number."

Katrina, barely awake, thanked Ron and took the flowers inside. She walked into the kitchen and found a vase to put them in which she filled halfway with water before walking back into the bedroom. Although she was curious to know who had sent her pink peonies, she assumed they were from a family member who had missed her wedding, and were meant to congratulate her on her marriage. As soon as her head hit the pillow, she fell into a deep sleep.

It wasn't until Katrina felt movement on the opposite side of the bed that she awoke. She reached for her cellphone on the bedside table and saw that it was 11:25 a.m., which meant that she had overslept. Both she and Marco had taken the day off from work to look at condos. She wondered why he hadn't woken her an hour earlier and turned to face his side of the bed where she saw him sitting upright, holding the card that had accompanied the flowers. "I have no idea who the flowers are from," she said, rubbing her eyes.

Marco opened the card and read it aloud. "Katrina, I've missed you so badly that I requested my New York route back. Please call me. I'll be there next month."

Stunned, Katrina's eyes widened. "I was wrong. I know who that's from."

"His phone number is written here. It looks like a French mobile. His name is Simon," said Marco.

Katrina felt that it was best to be honest. "Simon was the man I dated before meeting you. He cheated on me with another woman. I told him I'd never take him back and I meant it," she said.

Marco laughed. "Oh, is that it? It's okay honey. He's still smitten though, it appears," he said.

Katrina took the card from Marco, tore it up, and handed the pieces back to him. "I'll take a shower now."

"Okay, sweetheart," said Marco, placing what was left of the torn-up card on the bedside table.

In front of Marco, Katrina had remained calm, but she was unnerved by Simon's card. Her heart pounded in her chest as she entered the shower. She hoped that Simon wouldn't drop by her building and prayed that if he ever did, she and Marco would have moved into their new condo by then. After she finished her shower and changed into the dress she planned to wear that day, she walked into the kitchen and saw Marco sitting at the table eating breakfast. He had placed the flowers in the middle of the table. "I thought they were pretty," he said, looking up at her.

"They are," said Katrina, deciding that she would give them to her neighbor, Janet across the hall when she and Marco stepped out that afternoon.

Carmen's Breakup

Carmen, a thirty-three-year-old student working towards her Master's in Communication at the University of Miami, worked at the reception desk of the Diamante Hotel three nights a week. She met her boyfriend of two and a half years, Jason, a forty-four-year-old sports agent, when he was a guest at the hotel. Originally from Dallas, he had moved to Miami for work and bought a condominium next to the Palm Bay Yacht Club on the waterfront.

Carmen would often recall her first few encounters with Jason, and how she had kept a professional distance whenever he stayed at the Diamante, even though he had flirted with her shamelessly. Noticing her offish stance, it wasn't until he bought his condo and informed her that he would no longer be a guest that he'd handed her his business card. She remembered that day well – Jason, looking posh in a navy suit, smiled at her; his chestnut-brown hair flecked with golden highlights fell into his eyes as he spoke, which he swept it back with his right hand, a gesture she had become accustomed to. Finding him attractive and unable to get his image out of her mind, Carmen called him a week later, and they began dating.

Dating Jason had its advantages. He took Carmen to the best restaurants in town and to glamorous events where she met famous athletes and their beautiful wives. It also had its disadvantages, one of them being that she had to spend a lot of money on clothes. At the beginning of their relationship, Jason had bought her dresses and handbags so that she would fit in wherever they went, but that was no longer the case and she now had to cover the costs herself. There was also what she jokingly referred to as the "shoe problem." Jason was exactly her height and didn't want her to tower over him, so she always had to wear kitten or mid-heels. Shoes of this height were hard to find in Miami, land of stiletto heels and platforms. So, whenever she would come across a pair that she thought might go well with an outfit, she felt inclined to snap them up - rarely was this style of shoe inexpensive. Carmen also had insecurities about her appearance that ended up eating into her finances. A natural brunette with an olive complexion, she felt that she looked more attractive as a blonde, and Jason agreed. She had tried coloring her hair herself, but with disastrous consequences. She'd ended up achieving a shade of platinum blonde that looked gray against her skin. But even worse, it began falling out in handfuls. Luckily, her hair recovered within a few months. And she was able to find a talented colorist who applied natural-looking low-lights and highlights in a way that allowed her to maintain her blonde locks, but without the damage. These visits to the salon were starting to add up at an unaffordable pace.

Carmen hoped that Jason would eventually ask her to marry him or at least ask her to move in with him so that they could spend more time together. But that never happened – in fact, she had recently begun noticing Jason pulling away from her. Even though he told her that he loved her, it was always before or after intimacy. During their first two years as a couple, Carmen had slept over at Jason's condo several nights a month. But over the last few months he had stopped inviting her over, choosing instead to spend the night at her apartment, but only once a week. Carmen, tired of schlepping a bag of clothes to and from Jason's condo, was pleased with this arrangement at first, but soon her intuition began nagging at her – her relationship seemed to be going backwards. Another thing that had her worried was that he'd stopped taking her to parties, and whenever they were together, they were alone.

Carmen was close to her mother and confided in her whenever she experienced troubles at work or in her relationships, and this time was no different. Her mother, Kelly, who lived in Vermont, would often call her. But communication was difficult because Carmen's schedule changed, sometimes unexpectedly. Tonight was a Tuesday, her day off, so she called her mother to speak with her about Jason. Kelly answered and placed the call on video-mode so that Carmen could see her, and Carmen did the same. "You're not working tonight? Uh-oh…something must be wrong," she said, noticing Carmen's downcast expression.

"Everything is fine at work, but I have Tuesday's off now," Carmen said. "I'm calling to let you know that. But also, I wanted to get your opinion about a problem I'm having with Jason."

"I thought you two were doing well. Your father and I both liked him when we met him last Christmas. But then, we only met him the one time. What's going on?"

Holding the phone at face-level, Carmen entered the kitchen, turned on the overhead light, and took a seat at a small breakfast table. "For several weeks now, I've been getting the feeling that he doesn't want me to come to his condo. He always comes over to my place instead, and he barely comes by anymore. My question is this: Why would he suddenly stop inviting me over?"

"Has he been acting differently?" Kelly asked, moving her head sideways, inquisitively.

"He acts the same towards me. But he hasn't taken me to any events in a long time. That's the only other major change," said Carmen.

"Have you looked up his name online recently or checked his social media accounts? Maybe he lost his job and doesn't want to tell you. He might be feeling stressed-out and wants more time to himself. Or, maybe his housekeeper quit, and he doesn't want you to see the mess he's living in. He might have a new friend he hangs out with and thinks that you won't like him, so he keeps you at a distance. It could be any number of things," said Kelly.

Carmen nodded. Her mother was right. "I think I'll look him up online now. I haven't done that since we first began dating. I felt secure, so I didn't think I needed to watch him in that way."

"I know what you mean. It feels like a sneaky thing to do. But in this case, maybe you'll find out something you didn't know before. You could always talk to him about it and simply ask him what's going on."

"I could, but would he be honest?"

"I don't know him well enough to answer that question. But, I'm sure it's nothing. It just feels like something."

"I hope you're right," said Carmen. "Anyway, over the next three months you can reach me on Tuesdays."

"Alright, sweetheart. Thank you for informing me. I'll leave you to your sleuthing," Kelly said, ending the call.

The minute Carmen finished the call with her mother she entered her bedroom, switched on her laptop, and began searching online for information about Jason. She noticed that on the social media page he used frequently there were photos of him standing next to two new clients who he had never mentioned to her. He had also added new photos and deleted others; the ones he had deleted were of her. Getting a queasy feeling in her stomach, Carmen placed her laptop on the bedside table and decided to lie down, hoping it would help her think clearly. Why had Jason deleted her photos? And why had he never mentioned the new athletes he was representing? Carmen considered contacting her mother again, but then decided against it because there was nothing new to tell her. If she was wrong about the vibe she was getting, and Jason turned out to be completely innocent, if she continued telling her mother that she suspected him of cheating or being indifferent towards her, her mother might no longer accept him. "How can I find out what the hell is really going on?" she said.

A week went by and Carmen didn't hear from Jason at all. Since she didn't have to work until the evening, she decided to drop by his condo to speak with him in the middle of the day. Jason spent most of his time at the office, but he would sometimes go home to shower and change clothes if he had a lunch meeting and needed to look extra-sharp. Hoping to catch him at home, she hopped into her car and drove to his condo.

Carmen pulled up in front of Jason's building and felt lucky to have found a parking space close to the entrance. As she entered the lobby, she waved to the security guard who looked over at her, waved casually, and then went back to watching surveillance videos. Before reaching the elevators, she noticed a postal worker placing mail into slots and stopped in her tracks. Approaching the woman politely, she claimed that she lived in 1104 and asked if she would hand her the mail. The postal worker, having never seen her before, looked over at the security guard. When he looked back at her calmly and nodded, she took it as an indication that it was okay to hand the tall, clearly agitated blonde woman the mail to that unit. She then turned her back on Carmen and began filling other boxes.

Carmen stood in front of the boxes sorting through the letters. All were posted to Jason except for one. She read the name aloud, "Angela Castillo." She was about to approach the postal worker to inform her that she had put a letter in the wrong box, when she noticed that the address was correct. Placing the mail inside Jason's box and shutting it, she stood completely still, trying to figure out what was going on. Confused and desperate for more information, she approached the security guard. "I was going to head upstairs to see Jason, but I realized that he's probably still at the office. I know that Angela is staying here now. Do you know when she might be coming home? I'd like to speak with her, as well," she said.

"You're his personal assistant, right?" he said.

"Yes," said Carmen.

"I saw her leave this morning in a taxi with little Tony," he said. "She'll be back in the early evening."

"Tony?" said Carmen.

"Yes, you must have met him. He's Jason and Angela's boy," he said, casually. "His name is Anthony, but I call him Tony."

"I'll drop by later. Thank you," she said and exited the building. Stunned and shaking, she drove home.

When Carmen arrived back at her apartment, the first thing she did was switch on her laptop and look up Angela Castillo online. She found several in both Dallas and Miami and had to look through them all before finding the woman she felt would be the most likely to tempt Jason. Her eyes fell on the social media account of Angela Castillo-Erickson. No doubt that was her - Erickson was Jason's last name, and she recalled Jason telling her at the beginning of their relationship that he was divorced.

Angela had several social media accounts all of which contained photos and videos. In many of the photos she wore short cocktail dresses and glittery heels. Zooming in to get a look at her close-up, Carmen could see that she was busty and curvaceous. Her long black hair hung far past her shoulders, and her eyes, slicked with gobs of mascara, were an unnatural shade of green. "Fake boobs, fake hair, fake eyes, and fake nails," said Carmen, shaking her head.

Carmen placed Angela in her early forties – she had the vivaciousness of a girl in her twenties, but the confidence and over-the-top style of a wannabe jet-setter with two more decades under her belt. In nearly all of her photos, she stood with a group people. As her profession, she wrote that she was a "talent manager." Carmen assumed that she represented musicians because her videos featured different singers and bands playing. But it was a photo at the bottom of the page that drew Carmen's attention the most. In it, Angela was sitting in a garden on a white wicker sofa, smiling contently, her arms around a little boy. The boy, who she guessed was six or seven years old, resembled Jason.

Carmen zoomed in on Angela's hands, looking for a wedding ring, but no rings were on her fingers. This meant that after her divorce with Jason, she had never remarried. Wanting to know if there was something else she was missing in the puzzle that she was trying to piece together, Carmen checked Jason's social media accounts again, but there was no trace of Angela or his son. Wanting answers, Carmen called Jason. When he answered, she began speaking without allowing him to get a word in. "I dropped by your condo today. I found out that your ex-wife is staying with you." she said.

After making her statement, all Carmen heard on the other end was background noise – it sounded like he was at the car wash. After nearly a minute passed, she realized that she had stunned Jason into silence. Not hearing any response, she was about to hang up and call him again when he finally spoke. "My ex-wife lives in Dallas, but she's considering moving to Miami," he said.

"She lives with you," Carmen said. "I saw mail in her name."

"She doesn't," said Jason. "She has her own apartment that she's renting month-to-month. The mail you saw was probably from the school she wants our child to attend. It should have been addressed to me. If she moves here, I'll be able to spend time with Anthony."

"How long have you known that she was thinking of moving to Miami? You kept me in the dark. I don't even remember you ever mentioning a child," said Carmen.

"I told you when I first met you."

Carmen knew that she would have remembered something as important as that. However, on their first two dates, he had taken her to parties and she'd had a few drinks. It was possible that he had told her once without ever mentioning it again. "I don't recall that conversation."

"I want to see my son. That's all I'm thinking about."

"According to the security guard at your building, Angela comes and goes as she pleases, so she must have a key. Are you sleeping with her?"

"Why would you ask me that?"

Carmen thought it was strange that he answered her question with a question rather than denying it. "Why won't you answer my question?"

"She and Anthony have spent the night at my place a few times."

"Did you sleep with her?"

"She came into my room," said Jason. "But it only happened a couple of times."

"Of course, it did," said Carmen, fuming. "I am so stupid. For months, I knew that something was wrong. It was so obvious, but I was too naive to figure it out."

"She kept me from seeing Anthony for years. It was an ugly custody battle and she won. When she told me that she wanted to move to Miami, at first I didn't believe her. That's why I didn't say anything to you. I thought she wouldn't like it here and would head back to Dallas, but that's not what happened."

Carmen understood that divorce could be a painful and complicated process. She could forgive Jason for not telling her that Angela was considering moving to Miami, if he truly believed that she was unlikely to stay. But Jason had been unfaithful. "I'm happy for you that you now get to see your son. The problem is that you slept with someone else."

"So, what are you saying?"

"I'm saying that you've been sleeping with your ex-wife, so it's over between us." Just as she was about to end the call, she heard Jason stammering on the other end, attempting to negotiate with her. "This is non-negotiable!" she shouted. "So, don't think you can be slick with me, and don't waste your breath. We're through!"

Jason called Carmen twice during the first month after their argument and sent her apologetic chat messages. But Carmen, feeling betrayed, refused to take his calls or answer his messages. She had never heard of a divorced couple getting back together, but anything was possible. One thing was certain - Angela hadn't held a gun to Jason's head to get him to sleep with her – he had done it of his own free will. Another consideration was the best interest of the child. It would be healthiest for him to have both parents living in the same city, and ideal if his parents got back together. Although she had met Jason years after his divorce, she suddenly felt like the "other woman" in the situation.

Not wanting to face the pain of what had happened, Carmen threw herself into her work and studies. But when she sat in class during lectures, sometimes her mind would wander and she would think about Jason, causing her to miss critical information. To overcome this problem, she recorded the lectures and played them back to herself while studying at home. Concentrating at work wasn't easy either. Her job, that she normally enjoyed, suddenly felt taxing. She had always excelled at customer service; being friendly to guests came naturally to her. But in her state of mind, she resented the barrage of questions she fielded from visitors to the Diamante. Her manager took notice of her less than enthusiastic performance and approached her one evening as she handed a couple their room key cards. "What's with the sour expression?" he asked.

"It's nothing. I have a headache," she said, peering into her computer screen in, trying her best to appear busy.

"You must have had the same headache for days now," he said. "Are you ill?"

"No, I'm fine. I'll perk up," she said, looking over at him, a fake smile plastered on her face.

"Have a cup of coffee when you get a chance, and take some pain medication," he suggested, before walking into the office behind her and closing the door.

Carmen was relieved that the discussion with her manager ended on a neutral note and began smiling her best fake smile at work. Guests seemed unable to differentiate between a real and phony smile, or if they did, they were too polite to call her out on it.

By the second month after her breakup with Jason, Carmen began to feel the full brunt of her loss. When she'd ended her relationship, she told herself that she was young, had her whole life ahead of her, and that she would surely meet someone new in the near future. The problem was that in her heart she didn't want anyone else - she only wanted Jason. Even though he had betrayed her, she was still deeply in love with him. She found herself crying late at night before going to sleep, and had difficulty eating. When she noticed that her clothes began to feel looser, she was pleased, but when she became hypoglycemic in class more than once and had to run to a vending machine to buy a candy bar, she thought that maybe it wasn't such a good thing after all. It wasn't until she saw how gaunt her face looked in the mirror that she stepped onto the scale one morning and realized the extent of her weight loss. To get her toned, muscular figure back, she began drinking protein shakes and working out at the gym in her building. These workouts pepped her up emotionally, so she started to go regularly.

One evening, while running on the treadmill, Jason entered her mind, causing her to lose her footing. She tripped, scrambled backwards, and fell off the machine. Dazed and splayed awkwardly on the floor, she found herself on her back, wincing in pain. The coolness of the air conditioning on her skin somehow made the pain worse. Groaning and swearing, she opened her eyes and looked up. Looking down at her, a concerned expression on his face, was a handsome man in his twenties wearing a yellow t-shirt and navy track pants. "Are you alright?" he asked. "I've never seen anyone do that before."

Carmen attempted to stand up, but felt pain in her left knee and hip. Falling back onto the floor she said, "I'm fine, I think. But, I'll have to take my time getting up."

The man lent her his arm and helped her to her feet. "I'll bring you some ice," he said. Carmen noticed that he was looking her over like a medic, and guessed, by assessing his physique, that he was a professional athlete who understood sports injuries. Once he determined that she could stand upright on her own, he exited the gym. Five minutes later, he returned with an ice pack and found her leaning up against a wall, still grimacing in pain.

The man got down on his knees to look at her knee and applied the ice pack. "Hold it here firmly, but not too firmly," he directed her, guiding her hand to the correct area. "Actually, I think it's better if you keep it raised."

Carmen looked down at his sandy-blonde hair and tanned muscular arms. Finding him attractive, she continued to study him and didn't look away. Seeming to realize that she was checking him out he looked up at her and smiled, his hazel eyes, the color of honey, fixated on hers. His polite demeanor and kindness towards her calmed her and reassured her that she would be alright. "I think my knee is already becoming numb," she said.

"I'd suggest that you sit in that chair over there and elevate your leg," he said, pointing to a chair next to a desk in the farthest corner of the room.

Following his directions, Carmen hobbled over to the chair, lifted her leg, and balanced the ice pack on her knee. The pain in her hip was already starting to go away, thankfully. "I'm Carmen, by the way," she said, looking over at him. "You're very kind for helping me."

"I'm Jason. I'll be over there lifting weights," he said, pointing to the middle of the room. "But if you need me, just shout."

"I will. Thank you again," she said. Of all the names in the world, he had to be named Jason. Disappointed and promising herself that she would never say that name ever again, she focused her attention exclusively on her knee.

Driving home from work on a Monday evening, Carmen heard her cellphone ring. Fumbling through her handbag she found it and quickly glanced at it. Seeing

184

that it was Jason, she pulled over to the side of the road to take the call. "Hello Jason. What do you want?"

"How are you?" he said, quietly.

"I'm fine. Did Angela move to Miami with Anthony?"

"Yes."

Carmen could hear background noise and guessed that Jason was at a busy restaurant. "Are you still sleeping with her?" she asked.

"She's the mother of my son," he said. "She's a big part of my life."

This was not the answer that Carmen wanted to hear. "I guess I'm not the type of woman who can handle something like this. If you're still attracted to her, you should remarry her and live together with your son. I'm not going to play the second wife, so you'll have to cut me loose."

"Can you give me time to figure out what I want to do?"

"Take all the time in the world, but don't expect me to be waiting," she said. When Jason said nothing, she ended the call.

Tossing her phone into her handbag, Carmen drove back onto the road. Tears streamed down her face as she thought about the beautiful moments she'd shared with Jason and how much she still loved him. When she arrived home, she looked at her phone again and saw a missed call from her mother, so she called her back. "Jason just called me. I'm a wreck," she said, turning the video-mode on.

"Is he still sleeping with his ex-wife?"

Carmen shrugged her shoulders. "I believe so. He didn't admit it outright, but he didn't tell me they weren't having sex either."

"It must be a difficult situation for him. He loves his child and is attracted to his ex, but he knows that things probably won't work out a second time, so he doesn't want to risk remarrying her."

"And I'm just supposed to sit on the sidelines and watch this play out?"

Kelly shook her head. "No, you shouldn't have to do that. I know it hurts, but you have no choice but to go on with your life and put him behind you. There's nothing you can do. It's not just him making the decisions, it's also Angela. If she sees that he isn't fully interested, she might start dating again. But this situation could drag on for months or even years."

"I wonder if she knows that I even exist," said Carmen. "Maybe he never told her about me."

"It's irrelevant. This has nothing to do with you."

"Should I contact her through social media?"

Carmen's mother paused and looked at her sternly. "Why would you do that? It would be pointless. What are you going to do, compete with her for this man's attention? Jason would love that - what an ego-boost that would be. Don't you understand that he's putting you on ice until *he* decides what he's going to do? You made the right decision. If Angela tires of waiting for him to fully commit to her, or she meets another man, then you and Jason would be in the clear, but that might never happen. Or, it could happen years from now. The worst part about this situation is that he cheated on you. Your father never cheated on me, and no men in the family have cheated on their wives accept for your uncle Mel and cousin Sam, and look what a mess they made of their lives."

Carmen's eyes welled with tears. "I love him so much. It hurts badly, and I feel so helpless."

"I know it does, sweetheart. Unfortunately, he's a liar and a cheater. Let him go. You'll find someone better."

Carmen nodded. "That's what I'm hoping…one day."

"It will happen. Just try to stay focused on other things."

After ending the call with her mother, Carmen entered the bathroom and washed off what little makeup remained on her face after having cried. She prayed that her mother was right.

As the weeks passed, Carmen's pain and anger began to subside. She attributed this to the fact that she had kept herself busy. However, because she had spent so much time working and studying, she hadn't gone to the gym in a long time. Wanting to stay healthy, she decided to start working out again.

On a Friday evening, when she arrived home from work, she changed into a tank top and shorts, hopped onto the elevator, and headed downstairs to the gym. As she reached the bottom floor she looked at her cellphone for the time and realized that it would be closing in half an hour. Telling herself that a few minutes on the treadmill was better than nothing, she entered. To her surprise there were several people there, all men, mostly in their forties - she guessed that the only time they had to exercise was after they got home from the office. As she walked towards the treadmills, she saw Jason, the man who had given her an ice pack for her knee, bench pressing in the middle of the room. Another man stood over him, spotting him. She immediately noticed that he was wearing the same yellow t-shirt as the night they met. When he took a short break and sat up, she waved to him as she hopped on the treadmill.

Jason rose to his feet, while his friend assisted him in unracking the weight. He then poured himself a cup of water at the cooler, and walked over to Carmen. "Your name is Carmen, correct?"

"You got it," she said, changing the incline on the treadmill. "Why do you like the color yellow so much?" she asked, pointing to his shirt.

"Blue and yellow are the colors of my alma mater," he answered.

Carmen had seen Jason in the gym twice after the day he'd helped her but chose not to speak with him. Both times his attention had been on his workout, so she had used the treadmill, lifted some free weights, and left without saying a word. She hadn't used the gym in such a long time that she had all but forgotten about him. "I'm sorry I didn't speak to you the last couple of times I was here. My boyfriend and I broke up and I was in a lousy mood," she said.

"I understand," he said. "My girlfriend and I broke up a month ago. It was a long-distance relationship that wasn't working out. Breakups are always a downer."

Carmen smiled and nodded. She had been so obsessed with her own situation that it hadn't occurred to her that other people around her might be going through the same thing. Jason stood silently next to the treadmill, holding onto the handrail and looking up at the television on the wall. She couldn't help but stare at him. Normally, a sweaty man would have turned her off, but she found Jason incredibly attractive. "Can I call you Jay," she asked. "I mean, instead of Jason."

He turned to look at her. "No one has ever called me Jay before, but I guess it's okay."

"My ex is named Jason," she said, hitting the slowdown button.

Jason burst out laughing. "So, that's why you never talked to me again."

"I wasn't even sure that you knew I was in the same room with you," she said.

"I knew," he said, smiling.

"Are you hungry?" she asked.

Jason was surprised by the question. "I'm always hungry," he said. "Why do you ask?"

"I was going to order a pizza. Do you want to come over to my place when you're done with your workout? I know that it's almost 10 o'clock, but I haven't eaten since lunchtime."

Jason's eyes widened, as if Carmen had asked him to do something naughty. "Sure, I can drop by in an hour. What's your apartment number?"

"It's 504," she said.

That night Jason came over to Carmen's apartment, and after taking only a few bites of pizza, they ended up kissing on the sofa. When she brought out a bottle of wine, Jason drank three glasses. Losing his inhibitions, he attempted to climb on top of her, but Carmen resisted. "We will, but just not on a first date," she said.

"We've technically known each other for a few months," he said, leaning against the back of the sofa, composing himself.

"True, but I was talking about an actual date."

"Fair enough," he said. "As long as kissing isn't off limits."

* * *

After hitting it off on their first date, Carmen and Jason began seeing each other. When she asked him what he did for a living, he explained that he was a former athlete, and that a serious injury that hadn't healed properly kept him from playing football. So instead of following that career path, he was studying kinesiology and wanted to open his own gym. Carmen categorized him as "The other Jason" in her mind, so that saying his name wouldn't upset her.

Late on a Tuesday evening, lying in bed next to Jason, Carmen heard her cellphone ring. Her head on his chest and in a blissful state of mind, she didn't want to answer, but Jason insisted. "It's probably your mother. It's rude not to talk to her," he said.

Reaching under the bed, she picked her phone up off the floor and saw that Jason was right. She answered, putting the call speakerphone. "Mom, I can't put the video on for a number of reasons. But, how are you?"

"I'm fine. The question is, how are you?"

"I'm with Jason. We're hanging out at my place. We'll probably watch a move in a few minutes," Carmen said.

"You've taken back that cheating bastard? Why would you do that?" Kelly said.

Carmen looked at Jason, now sitting up in bed, a severe expression on his face. "Mom, I'm talking about the guy I met at the gym. Don't you remember? I told you all about him."

"And his name is Jason too? That doesn't bode well."

"They have the same name but they're not the same person," said Carmen. When she heard no response she said, "Mom, are you there?"

"Your father just walked in through the back door. I think he injured himself fixing the car. I have to go now, sweetheart. Go and watch your movie. I'll ring you back later," said Kelly, ending the call.

Carmen switched her phone off and placed it back on the floor. She looked over at Jason who was shaking his head. "You'd better just call me Jay so that we don't have any problems."

"I'm sorry," said Carmen.

"It's fine. No worries," said Jason, holding her close.

Chapter Sixteen

Reconditioning Yourself to Dating

After a failed relationship you might feel war weary, like you've fought hard but lost the battle. It's not easy to get back out there and try again. If you're out of practice because you've just come out of a long relationship, dating can be intimidating. You're putting your ego on the line, hoping for a mutual attraction with someone you find desirable. At the same time, you're wary whenever you meet someone new. Even if things go well, when a new man enters your life changes take place and adjustments need to be made. Not everyone can do this with ease. If you're not quite ready, take your time and gradually start going out more. Be open to meeting men, but don't make it your number one priority. Go out and have fun with friends or by yourself.

Don't Allow People to Categorize You Based on Your Age

There's nothing more annoying than when a friend or family member tells you that you missed your chance and should have gotten married at a certain age. Your life doesn't have to unfold in perfect harmony with other people's expectations. People can't plan their lives around their age, and opportunities come around at different times in life. Perhaps, in some instances being too young is a problem. But you're never too old to do anything, be it start a business, go back to school, or meet the right partner.

Remain Open to Making Friends with a Variety of People

When you only socialize with people in your age group, or you only go out with co-workers or people attending your same university, you limit your options in life. People meet their significant others and make new friends in all sorts of ways. If you're in your thirties and a woman living in your building is in her fifties, but you have a lot in common, there's no reason why you shouldn't befriend her and plan activities with her that you're both interested in. The point is that you should be out of the house doing interesting things and having a good time. It's possible that when you're out enjoying yourselves, a man you find attractive will approach you. This might happen at a restaurant, museum, art gallery, farmers market, clothing store, the gym, or any number of places. The same thing can happen to her if she's single and is open to meeting someone. Also, keep in mind that your friend from your building might have a relative or acquaintance you find attractive, so keep her in the loop and have fun hanging out together when you're both interested in the same activity.

Have Patience and Reasonable Expectations

When choosing a partner, their physical appearance counts of course, but you shouldn't limit yourself by sticking to a particular "type" only. Do you tend to reject men who you don't feel an immediate attraction to? If this is your dating pattern, keep in mind that real love takes time to develop. Passionate romances that occur quickly often burn out just as quickly. Don't expect a man to rock your world when you first meet him. When you like someone as a person and enjoy his company, a spark might come later. Being patient has its rewards. A slow growing romance that starts with friendship can lead to an exciting, passionate relationship.

Never Waste Your Time

It's never wise to invest all your energy in a person who gives you conflicting signals, or indicates that they're not interested in being in a committed relationship. Unless the relationship becomes serious, date others. This way of thinking will protect you from wasting your time. Oftentimes, women feel guilty about even considering dating other men, even if their relationship is a casual one that is clearly not progressing, thinking that doing so would be disloyal. If you continue to date someone exclusively who isn't interested in having a real relationship with you and keep yourself closed to other men, the only one you're being disloyal to is yourself.

Getting Over Disappointment and Trust Issues

For some, the disappointment of being betrayed or losing the affections of someone they love is so great that they are unable to bounce back and date again. They would rather be alone than potentially put themselves through the trauma of another heartbreak. These feelings are understandable. However, when this becomes your attitude, what you're doing is giving the person who hurt you the power to destroy your trust in people. The world is full of men who will not betray you, and are trustworthy and kind. But if you don't allow them access you'll never come to that realization. To counter trust issues, take baby steps when you meet a man – take your time getting to know him slowly.

Using Dating Sites

A great way to meet men is through friends, at a party with people you know, or even through work because you at least have some background on them. Another good way is to hang out in your neighborhood

– at the gym, a coffeehouse, restaurant, local event, or even the grocery store. But if you feel that you're not meeting enough men in your daily life, you might want to try dating sites. What's wonderful about these sites is that you don't have to get dolled-up constantly and go to parties, events, or nightclubs in an attempt to meet men – you can do it from the comfort of your home or while walking around town doing errands, and checking your cellphone occasionally. Although there are lots of players on these sites, it's possible to find a potential marriage partner this way. If you hear through the grapevine that a certain site has gained a reputation for casual hookups, you can switch to a different site because there are plenty to choose from.

One of the downsides of dating sites is that they give people the perception that they have never- ending choices, so they often feel little empathy towards people they interact with. Also, when looking at profiles, people tend to judge others mainly on their appearance. The problem with this is that some people are more adept at photographing themselves than others – they know about lighting and angles – so a good-looking man might take a photo that makes him look less attractive than he is, and visa versa. It can be difficult to gauge your attraction to someone who is not standing in front of you, so you might choose wrongly and miss the opportunity to meet someone that in real life you would find interesting. Another problem is that people tend to set parameters that limit them – you might state in your profile that you want to meet a man who is within a certain age range and miss out on meeting someone that happens to be a bit older or younger who you might have had more in common with.

If you decide to delve into this way of meeting men, keep in mind that most people have good days and bad days while utilizing these sites. If you're concerned that the person you wish to meet might be different than what you were hoping for, you can always plan a quick video call before setting up a formal date to make sure that both of you have the desire to move forward.

You can walk away altogether and stop using dating sites if they make you uncomfortable. Most people still meet their significant others in traditional ways, even though the number of people using dating sites continues to grow. Meeting someone online works for people who are very driven to find someone, and who can accept rejection as well as reject others without becoming anxious during the process.

Approach Men and Be Approachable

One of the reasons that people ping-pong in and out of low-quality relationships with their exes is because they don't actively try to meet new people. Shyness and the fear of being rejected or misunderstood are the main causes. It's difficult to break this negative pattern of thinking, but it can be done.

Learn to pay attention to your surroundings when you're out of the house doing errands, going to and from work, or wherever else you find yourself frequently, rather than staring into your cellphone. Once you are aware of what's going on around you, you will notice people more, including men who you might find attractive. The old techniques of attention-getting and seduction are still as effective as ever –

people have become so accustomed to staring into screens that they've forgotten these basics. Glance in his direction, behave in a subtle yet flirtatious way, or you can even simply stand next to him and politely smile, indicating that if he's interested in starting a conversation, you would be open to it - do whatever has worked for you in the past. If the man you're interested in meeting doesn't begin a conversation with you, you can always start one with him. If you're standing next to an attractive man in line at a coffeehouse waiting to put in your order, you can casually ask him his opinion about a certain tea or coffee, or if he has tried it before. If you're at the gym, you can ask a man when he'll be done using the treadmill. If you get the feeling that he's interested, you can come up with any number of casual topics to talk with him about to set him at ease. If he finds you attractive, he'll automatically lengthen the conversation – that's your cue to hand him your business card. If he's curt with you, at least you tried. Smile politely, gear your mind towards something else, and walk away. And remember, there will be others.

Your Dates Don't Need to Know the Details of Your Breakup

During the dating process, a man will ask a woman personal questions to get to know her better. If the man you're on a date with asks you about your dating history, it's best to give him some basic details only, and not discuss the high and low points of your relationships, especially the breakup that devastated you the most. Remember, the man you're on a date with is not a confidante or girlfriend. He's someone you're interested in, and he is interested in you. You want him to imagine you in his arms, not the arms of another man. Men are keenly aware that women make comparisons, and this affects their confidence. Put the past out of your mind and instead, smile, be friendly, and get to know your date.

Looking for Good Character

When you decide to date again, make sure to always look for good character in a man. Recognizing and appreciating this will make your dating life a hundred times easier, and allow you to meet the quality person you deserve. Don't ignore your intuition when you know that someone is acting strangely or not treating you right. Some behaviors that scream RUN IN THE OTHER DIRECTION FAST are:

- When you met him, he told you that he was single. But later, you found out he had a live-in girlfriend or was married while he was dating you.

- He's hot and cold; he acts as if he's passionately in love with you, but then pulls away completely. You want a man who is sure that he wants to be with you, not someone who is ambivalent.

- He puts you down in front of others.

- He has destroyed his own credit and wants you to cosign for a large loan.

199

- He is obsessed with social networks, and uses them to check out all the hot women online. He regularly responds to messages he receives from ex-girlfriends on these sites, even though you have repeatedly asked him to stop. He refers to them as "just old friends," even though you've read some of these messages and can see that they are flirtatious.

- He sees any woman who is in a relationship with him as an extension of himself, rather than a separate person with her own needs, desires, and ambitions. His needs always come first.

- He's jealous and constantly accuses you of cheating or flirting with other men.

Look for Positive Behaviors Such As:

- He contacts you regularly. Even when he's super-busy, you'll pop into his mind throughout the day and he'll send you a chat message or ring you to say a quick hello.

- He's reliable; when you set a date and time to meet, he's there.

- He's honest; he doesn't need to lie because he's not hiding anything.

- He might not always agree with you, but he respects your opinions.

- He's faithful to you.

- He ignores ex-girlfriends and other women who attempt to contact him online, and focuses on your relationship.

Luck in Romance

Luck in romance can be achieved by being optimistic and confident. You need to be able to put yourself out there. If you get hurt or experience a setback, it's important to believe that it's only temporary and that luck will swing back in your favor. Improving romantic luck involves:

- Being upbeat and positive.
- Not harping on mistakes you feel you've made in your relationships. Try to avoid making the same mistakes in the future, but stop replaying them in your head endlessly.
- Looking forward to tomorrow's opportunities.
- Actively trying to meet someone. You cannot be *found* – that's not realistic. You've got to be out there and available.
- Respecting your own boundaries.
- Focusing on your strong points, not your weaknesses.
- Not allowing cultural beliefs to cripple you. Keep those beliefs that have helped you, and distance yourself from ways of thinking that have always worked against you.

- Accepting some risk in life. If you plan every detail you leave no room for luck. Luck involves some uncertainty…some volatility.
- Being willing to win or lose. If you don't try, you'll never know what the possibilities are.
- Wearing clothing and colors that look good on you, and make you feel great. You will exude confidence, making you a magnet for others.
- Being around people and making connections.
- Spending time with optimistic and successful people who see the possibilities in life.

Break-up Survival
Summaries

- If you've just come out of a long-term relationship you might feel out of practice when it comes to dating. Start by being more social.
- Don't put all your energy into someone who gives you mixed signals or doesn't want to be in a healthy, stable relationship. Don't close yourself off from meeting other men should the opportunity arise.
- Don't let disappointment and trust issues keep you from dating. But don't rush into a new romantic relationship; take your time getting to know someone.
- If you enjoy a man's company and are interested but not extremely attracted to him, try being patient and allowing a slow romance to develop. If it does that's great and if it doesn't, then so be it.
- Remember to always look for good character in a man.
- Romantic luck will come with positive thinking and action.
- If you haven't had the best luck lately, consider it temporary. You'll be lucky again.

Hopefully, after you've finished reading this book you'll be on your way to achieving your goal of getting over your breakup. And when you do, know that you have a world of options and wonderful things can happen for you. By remaining positive you can never lose.

About the Author:
Susanna Gold is a writer whose main focus is love, romance, dating, and relationships. She divides her time between Los Angeles and London.

Made in the USA
Coppell, TX
21 December 2020